Apr...

C students;
ork, self-confiden...

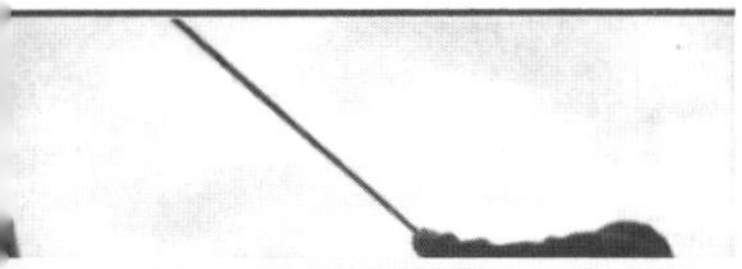

Civil engineering program
back by popular demand

BY LANCE SOUTHWORTH
ASSISTANT EDITOR

Back before a lot of us ever thought about going to college, LCC was named The Lexington Technical Institute. This institute offered a civil engineering associate degree that trained students to have the basic knowledge to equip them to ...

offer many general education classes that are familiar to students. Nineteen full-time faculty members will be on board at the new facility.

Of the amenities offered at the campus, Roberts said "It'll be an opportunity for students to go to a site and do everything at that site." He said the campus offerings will include registration, counseling, a bookstore, a computer lab with internet access, a lounge area and vending. The school hopes these features, as well as the campus's location, will be a draw for students who often have a hard time getting the classes they want at the times they want.

According to Roberts, South Campus can handle an enrollment of 300-350 students initially. LCC currently has about 7,200 students. LCC

See SOUTH CAMPUS pg. 4

engineering of sites like: The Lexington Legends Stadium, Tates Creek and Palomar Centers, RiteAide sites all over the country, and the McCreary County Federal Prison. The mechanical engineers at GRW were responsible for the upgrade of UK Commonwealth Stadium.

Slugantz mentioned with that the high drop-out rate at UK in the Civil Engineering Program, this gives students a different avenue.

"Fifty percent to 60 percent of the freshmen drop out within the first year and 10 percent to 15 percent of transfer students to UK drop out," according to Dr. George Blandford, director of undergraduates in civil engineering.

Only students with a four-year degree from UK can become a registered engineer in the state of Kentucky. But the tech program can be a step up the ladder.

To smoke or not to smoke

Doorway puffing could be banned

By KURTIS LEDFORD
Courier Staff

Smokers could lose their chance for a between-class cigarette in front of LCC buildings - no ifs, ands or butts about it.

The doorways to the Moloney Building (MB), the Oswald Building (OB) and the Academic Technical building (AT) are permeated by smoke, which everyone must navigate on their way to and from class.

Kurt Wujcik (left) and Patrick Malon...

three major issues that need ... addressed in the smoking debate:

-- There technically are only three designated smoking areas -- on the stadium side of the OB, on the Atrium patio, the Cooper ...

Campus relieves growing pains

...ON

...: It's regis-
...n, class that
...schedule is
...o?
...ster for that
...new South
...what LCC

...CC will be-
...mpus at the
...enrolled in
...es at LCC's
...first to ex-
...the new fa-
...move there

...nt Dean of
...he decision
...us, which is

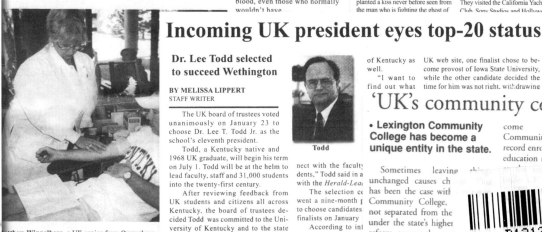

The South Campus will take over the former Sullivan College building on Regency Road.
Photo by Ferran Robinson

under a three-year lease, was a result of limited space at LCC due to a continually growing enrollment. The East Campus, also leased, will continue to host non-credit courses.

When spring 2001 registration begins, all new and returning students will have the opportunity to attend classes at the South Campus. According to Roberts, the South Campus will

...and wastewater management.

John Slugantz, project ma... for the local firm GRW Engineers, graduated from LTI back in '84 bef... tech program was discontinued.

"Knowledge and applicati... wise, it is the same as UK," says Sl... referring to the ability of this new p... gram. The program at UK is calcul... based; LCC's program will be trigo... etry-based.

GRW has been credited w...

LCC's SIFE hits a home run for Legends basebal...

BY TONY CORD
STAFF WRITER

Lexington is finally getting its own pro baseball team. The stadium is already under construction and the team's web site is up and running. The sale of Legends-related merchandise, however, could have been a different story.

The LCC chapter of SIFE – Students In Free Enterprise – will be pitching in to help open the fledgling team's store.

"This just happened to fall into our laps," said Virginia Fairchild, the head of the award-winning LCC- based SIFE team.

As it turns out, the original merchandiser pulled out at the last minute to take a more profitable offer. T'm Brauer, of the Lexing-

ton Legends marketing staff and a former student of Fairchild's, stopped by and spoke to her abo...

the store's difficulties. Seeing an opportunity for SIFE to help, she immediately offered to lend a hand.

When the Legends r... opens in Turfland mall, sev... members and students in l... retail management class he... will be there seeing how ... prise works first hand whil... the store come into its ow...

SIFE is a non-profit or... ganization interested in h... members obtain experience... enterprise, while teaching... example and community ... programs. SIFE is open to ... students who wish to join. ... interested, SIFE meets ev... at noon in AT 102.

Interested in Lexington ... Baseball? Visit the ... www.lexprobaseball.co...

...al hygiene
...nt wins
... Bean
...Radiology
...d.
...page 7.

LCC students and faculty watch coverage of the Sept. 11 attacks, give their reactions. See page 3.

...at LCC
See page 10.

COURIER

...lume 5, Number 1   September 2001

...exercise in eastern
...met at Barker Hall on
...t 5 a.m. From there

American town, to an ambush... far away East Asian jungle. A... each situation the cadets are t...

Plymire said he enrolled in ROTC to earn a ... his first year of law school. He plans to contin... gram and to become involved with JAG.

Photos by Reia...

News
October 2000

Professor introduces LCC to the DNC

BY THERESA STANLEY
CO-EDITOR

LCC Political Science Professor Tim Cantrell participated in the 2000 Democratic National Convention in Los Angeles. As a Kentucky delegate, he received a ground-floor view of the activities.

Spectators will remember the overwhelming excitement of Al Gore as he stepped up to the platform to deliver the speech of his lifetime. He pulled Tipper close to him and planted a kiss never before seen from the man who is fighting the ghost of

by his party to represent our state at the national level on the ground floor of the four-day convention. While on the floor, Cantrell ran into a former LCC student, Susan Westrom, who is now a Kentucky Democratic Representative from Fayette County.

Cantrell, his wife and other delegates spent five days with Ky. Governor Paul Patton and his wife. They visited the California Yacht Club, Sony Studios and Hollywood ...

Democrats know how to party

Tim Cantrell stopped to chat with former LCC student and State Representative Susan Westrom (D-Fayette). The smiles convey the participants' level of excitement over the activities at the 2000 Democratic National Convention.
Photo submitted

...nts roll up sleeves to help

...attacks inspire donors to give at blood drive

...tional
...eft,
...id

...e
...y
...y
...s

...success, every-
...stacles and bar-
...tional student
...glish, just drop
...30-1:30 in MB
...glish skills.

blood, even those who normally wouldn't have...

Stacey Sutton

...ou through the
...ng from the ba-
...anced compre-
...g vocabular-
... It is a special
...nal students to
...eriences with
...r parts of the

...atthew Winpelberg, a UK senior from Owensboro, ... to give blood from 10:30 a.m. until 2:30 p.m. Elizabe... Central Kentucky Blood Center, took Winpelberg's contribution.

Incoming UK president eyes top-20 status

Dr. Lee Todd selected to succeed Wethington

BY MELISSA LIPPERT
STAFF WRITER

The UK board of trustees voted unanimously on January 23 to choose Dr. Lee T. Todd Jr. as the school's eleventh president.

Todd, a Kentucky native and 1968 UK graduate, will begin his term on July 1. Todd will be at the helm to lead faculty, staff and 31,000 students into the twenty-first century.

After reviewing feedback from UK students and citizens all across Kentucky, the board of trustees decided Todd was committed to the University of Kentucky and to the state

Todd

of Kentucky as well.

"I want to find out what ...

...nect with the faculty ...
...dents," Todd said in a ...
...with the *Herald-Lea...*

The selection c... went a nine-month p... to choose candidates ... finalists on January ...

According to inf...

UK web site, one finalist chose to become provost of Iowa State University, while the other candidate decided the time for him was not right, withdrawing ...

'UK's community college' enjoying sing...

• **Lexington Community College has become a unique entity in the state.**

Sometimes leaving ...hi... unchanged causes ch... has been the case wit... Community College, ... not separated from the ... under the state's higher ... reform, as were the state ... community colleges.

To begin with, the ... change in enrollment. LCC set a new record this fall with 6,110 students, an increase of 9.38 percent over last academic year. That number includes students from 108 Kentucky counties, 36 U.S. states and 23 foreign countries. LCC

come from Hopkinsville Community College – credits the record enrollment in part to higher education reform, which left LCC ...

Chain of command

LCC's unchanged status also is causing changes in administration. No longer reporting to a community college chancellor, the college also does not answer to the Kentucky Community and ...

leges do. The result is ... more autonomy and ... new people to an ... University Senate ... force is reviewing a ... rules. In some cases ... will change rules, whi... of administrative rules... recommendations t... Charles T. Wething... will submit changes ... of Trustees.

"That doesn't mean ... have to change. It's a r... There may be changes ... the University wants t... Roy Moore, chair of t... Senate, which now incl... members from LCC.

An example of ch...

...mmunity stunned by events of Sept. 11

...forever be
...kest days

second plane crash, American Airlines Flight 77 was crashed into the U.S. Pentagon in Washington, D.C. Twenty minutes after the Pentagon attack, another airliner, United Airlines Flight 93 crashed in Pennsylvania, about 80 ...

could simply not believe what they were witnessing.

"I was in a total state of disbelief," said Lori Guiseppi, an English professor at LCC. "At first, I thought it was just a devastating plane crash. I felt so bad for ...

instructor Leon Lane, were not so surprised. "I was not shocked," said Lane. "No one who studies world affairs would be. I was surprised by the scale of the attack and the method in which it was carried out, but not by the fact that we were a target of terrorism ...

D1212830

The University of Kentucky

1965–2005

Lexington Community College

The University of Kentucky
1965–2005
Lexington Community College

A Pictorial History

Rick Smoot

The Donning Company Publishers
184 Business Park Drive, Suite 206
Virginia Beach, VA 23462

Brad Martin, Project Director

Steve Mull, General Manager
Barbara Buchanan, Office Manager
Pamela Koch, Senior Editor
Mellanie Denny, Graphic Designer
Derek Eley, Imaging Artist
Cindy Smith, Project Research Coordinator
Scott Rule, Director of Marketing
Tonya Hannink, Marketing Coordinator

Library of Congress Cataloging-in-Publication Data

Smoot, Rick, 1956–
  The University of Kentucky Lexington Community College, 1965-2005:
a pictorial history / by Rick Smoot.
        p. cm.
  Includes bibliographical references and index.
  ISBN-13: 978-1-57864-473-5 (hard cover : alk. paper)
  1. Lexington Community College--History. 2. Lexington Community
College--Pictorial works. I. Title.
  LD6501.L49S64 2008
  378.768'21
                    2007047888

Printed in the United States of America at Walsworth Publishing Company

Acknowledgments

Many people helped make this book possible. I am grateful for the foresight demonstrated by Dr. A. James Kerley, president of the University of Kentucky Lexington Community College, who understood the importance of preserving the unique history of the College for all those touched by it. For reading the manuscript in various stages of development, I am most grateful for the comments of Dr. Sandy Carey, dean of academic affairs at Bluegrass Community and Technical College, and Bluegrass colleagues Professors Peggy Saunier, Joanne Olson-Biglieri, and David Wachtel. John Adams's interviews with current and former faculty and administrators contributed to the narrative. For inspiration I thank Mr. Geoffrey Morgan, a good friend and a good Englishman. For technical assistance I thank Mr. Michael Brendan Riggs, another friend and former student, and Ms. Tonya Spivey, who never turned down a single request for photocopies I made, no matter how inconvenient for her. Thanks to Mr. Frank Stanger of the University of Kentucky Special Collections and Digital Programs for his help. Additional assistance came from Ms. Beverly Drake, both in reading materials and contributing information.

Others who read the drafts of the manuscript and offered their insights include Peter P. Bosomworth, M.D., Charles T. Wethington, Jr., Ph.D., Professors Art Dameron, Patrick McDermott, and Charles Coulston. Librarians Charles James and Steve Stone and History Professor Steven J. White contributed vital information to the work. Charles James also is to be commended for his contribution of many images used throughout the text. Professor Bill Batson also made images available. Professor Tammy Ramsey and the *Courier* proved quite helpful in terms of articles and images. Ms. Marilyn Childre and Ms. Vern Kennedy assisted in identification of images and in comments on the manuscript. Many, many others assisted me at various stages of writing and preparation of the work at hand but remain anonymous because of space restrictions. You know who you are, and I thank you.

During the writing of this book I lost my very best friend in the world, my canine companion Heffner. Heff, I couldn't have done any of it without you; I love you and miss you.

Contents

◀ Looking toward the UK campus
from the Oswald Building (right).

▲ Directions to the offices of the University of Kentucky Community
College System and to the Lexington Technical Institute.

Prologue

This is a history of the institution known officially from 1965 to 1983 as the University of Kentucky Lexington Technical Institute (LTI), and then called officially from 1984 to 2004 the University of Kentucky Lexington Community College (LCC). This history project was undertaken as a result of the fortieth anniversary of the College in 2005, and in consideration of the looming change in governance from the University of Kentucky (UK) to the Kentucky Community and Technical College System (KCTCS) that occurred in 2004–2005. Before the history and many achievements of the College were lost, this formal, albeit brief, history of the College in words and images was created.

Here is an examination of LTI's and later LCC's relationship with its parent institution, the University of Kentucky. The work is arranged for the most part in a chronological fashion. Generally, the organization is within the context of the administrations of the Institute or College, either the director or president. In as many places as was practicable, the story progresses within the milieu of American national and Kentucky state higher education developments. It is a treatment that includes material both objective and subjective, as well as impressionistic and anecdotal. Space limitations and the very nature of the work, styled as "A Pictorial History," tells the reader that this does not pretend to be a comprehensive treatment in any way. Far more could be said, far more players named and placed, many more events examined and achievements hailed, were time and space available.

In the first chapter, "Present at the Creation," the early background of the University of Kentucky is given side by side with the history of the development of two-year postsecondary institutions in the United States and in Kentucky. The chapter proceeds to the development of state-supported community colleges in Kentucky,

their relationship with the University of Kentucky, and the creation of the Lexington Technical Institute by the University of Kentucky Board of Trustees. The progress of the LTI operation from inception to the mid-1970s rounds out the chapter.

An examination of the Institute's expansion comes in the second chapter, "Growing with the Times." From there we observe the progression of the school, ultimately moving from a strictly technical focus to a comprehensive community college, becoming more like the other UK community colleges statewide. With its new status came a new name: the University of Kentucky Lexington Community College. The story here goes as far as 1993, through the first two LCC administrations.

In the third chapter, "Still Bigger, Still Better," the theme is the continuing growth of the College and the overall progress of the programs and courses of study offered. Chapter four, "Celebration!" is a reference to a favorite word of LCC's last president, and a testament to the heights LCC had reached before the decision to remove the College from the governance of the University. The chapter heralds the achievements of the 1990s and on into the early twenty-first century, and concludes with some of the details of the change in governance, and an assessment of the overall feeling of the College, its faculty, staff, and student body to the new relationship. A final few words that examine the influence of LTI and LCC appear in the Epilogue.

Within the limitations of the piece, every effort has been made to include recognition of as many people, programs, events, and achievements as possible. Efforts were made to preclude errors and avoid omissions. What errors and omissions occurred necessarily remain my responsibility. For those affected, your indulgence is requested.

Present at the Creation

Lexington, Kentucky, is known as the horse capital of the world, the "Queen of the Bluegrass," the "Athens of the West," all fitting sobriquets for a very unique place on the map. Founded in 1775, its name echoes the opening battle of the American Revolution fought that April in Massachusetts. Thoroughbred horses flourish in the Bluegrass, as do fine standardbreds, raised on the strikingly beautiful horse farms that grace the countryside, manicured to perfection. Lexington was home to one of America's most important nineteenth-century statesmen, Henry Clay, "Harry of the West," the greatest of the Great Triumvirate. Lexington is also the birthplace of higher education west of the Allegheny Mountains, hometown to one of America's earliest colleges, founded in 1780 and named Transylvania.

It is that early connection to higher education to which attention here must be given. Lexington not only hosted Transylvania University, albeit called by a different name in certain years, most notably Kentucky University from 1865 until it reverted in 1908 to Transylvania. Lexington also is home to the University of Kentucky (UK), the land grant school of the Commonwealth, founded as Agricultural and Mechanical College in 1865, initially as a college of Kentucky University. The school evolved, as did its name, gained independent status in 1878, and later was renamed, in 1908, State University, Lexington, Kentucky. It arrived to its present designation on March 15, 1916, when, "without stating a reason," as UK historian and professor Carl Cone put it, the Kentucky General Assembly decided to rename it the University of Kentucky.

◄ Students stand in the quadrangle, with Breckinridge Hall in the background.

All the great land grant universities in the United States can trace their beginnings as such to passage of the 1862 Morrill Act, signed by President Abraham Lincoln, that created from scratch most of the state-supported agricultural and mechanical, or engineering, colleges around the country. Each grant provided 30,000 acres of land for each member of Congress who represented that state. Over the years, with additional legislation, and in various incarnations, more than seventy such schools were created.

Land grant schools were a great innovation of the nineteenth century, addressing directly a national need for skilled, well-educated engineers, military personnel, and agricultural professionals. Another great innovation emerging from that same time was the junior college. In the 1850s and 1860s, several prominent American educators wanted to establish junior colleges to be responsible for preparatory or "general education" course work for entering undergraduates, giving them the basic core or educational foundation they needed to progress on in the university. The university thereby could concentrate on upper division course work, research, and professional schools.

Yet another sector of society demanded attention. Merchants of various stripes and others involved in the many manifestations of commerce called for a trained workforce to meet the increasingly complex demands of business and industry. Perhaps some sort of new apprenticeship or internship could be created and coupled with basic or general studies for balance. In response, we see here the emergence of the community colleges, devoted to technical and semiprofessional education. Over the path of the twentieth century, the two designations of junior and community college moved toward each other so that by the 1970s they converged and became essentially interchangeable terms for two-year colleges. Two scholars of higher education, Arthur M. Cohen and Florence B. Brawer, in their study entitled *The American Community College* (4th edition, 2003), give a succinct definition of such institutions:

The American community college dates from the early years of the twentieth century. Among the social forces that contributed to its rise, most prominent were the need for workers trained to operate the nation's expanding industries; the lengthened period of adolescence, which mandated custodial care of the young for a longer time; and the drive for social equality, which supposedly would be enhanced if more people had access to higher education. Community colleges seemed also to reflect the growing power of external authority over everyone's life, the peculiarly American belief that people cannot be legitimately educated, employed, religiously observant, ill, or healthy unless some institution sanctions that aspect of their being. (Cohen and Brawer, 1)

Thus defined and charged, community and junior colleges began to appear in rapid succession around the country beginning in the early twentieth century, at first usually as private as opposed to public or state-sponsored institutions. Here, again, Lexington provided a first as host of Kentucky's original community college, one of the first nationally. (Joliet Junior College in Joliet, Illinois, founded in 1901 some forty miles from Chicago, is generally acknowledged as the first "community" college in America.) According to a student of community colleges, Larry Stanley, Hamilton College opened in 1903 as Kentucky's first community college, although it originated as Hocker Female College, founded in 1869. In 1877 Hocker was sold to a private holding company and in the process of institutional evolution was renamed for one of its major investors, William Hamilton of Woodford County, Kentucky. Then in 1903 Hamilton was acquired by Kentucky University, the name used by Transylvania University from 1865 to 1908, and was reorganized and served as that school's junior college until 1932 when it was merged completely with Transylvania University.

> **Two-year schools attempted to build a niche with two-year programs in that netherworld between high schools and four-year colleges and universities.**

In the interim between the turn of the twentieth century and the world-altering events of World War II, the colleges and universities of Kentucky experienced the changes facing the United States in much the same way as did similar institutions around the country. After American involvement in World War I, from 1917 to 1918, the growth of junior colleges began to accelerate nationally. One important development that assisted such growth came in 1920 when the American Association of Junior Colleges was founded in St. Louis. Junior colleges now had a national organization where ideas might be shared and concerns could be given voice.

One big issue that faced two-year colleges around the country involved the development of "semiprofessional" programs, roughly defined as courses of study somewhere between the trades and the professions, as explained by Steven Brint and Jerome Karabel in *The Diverted Dream: Community Colleges and the Promise of Educational Opportunity in America, 1900–1985* (1989). Two-year schools attempted to build a niche with two-year programs in that netherworld between high schools and four-year colleges and universities. They would receive help from an "unexpected boom" in enrollment during the Great Depression, running from the "Great Crash" in 1929 on Wall Street to American entry into World War II in December 1941. High unemployment and general affordability coupled with new programs made for impressive growth in two-year colleges, from approximately 56,000 students nationally in 1929 to nearly 150,000 by 1939.

Steady expansion in the various sorts of two-year schools, public and private, could be readily measured up to the outbreak of World War II, when more pressing needs required the total mobilization of the vast American economy and the American military would swell its ranks with most college-aged males, not to mention many college-aged females, as well as a large portion of faculty and staff. The halls of academe emptied. Enrollments dropped precipitously, and many colleges and universities were threatened with suspension of activities or actual closure. Some did close temporarily; some, permanently.

Then the war was over in 1945 and the postwar expansion came, full-throttle, and fueled growth all across the wide spectrum of primary, secondary, and postsecondary education. The baby boom generation filled classrooms, while the 1944 G.I. Bill (formally the Servicemen's Readjustment Act) provided for paid college or vocational education for millions of veterans, and vets flocked to the schools. Other government actions contributed to growth. Passage in 1946 of the Hill-Burton Act (formally the Hospital Survey and Construction Act) built not only community hospitals nationally but also academic health sciences centers on many college campuses, such as the University of Kentucky. Dr. Vannevar Bush, chief science advisor to the President of the United States, in his famed report *Science: The Endless Frontier* (1945) argued expansion of science and research—and the institutions that support such endeavors, like colleges and universities—were so important to the future of the country that they should be considered vital to American national security. With national security firmly attached to the various levels of the American educational enterprise, federal dollars flowed in quantities never before seen, building a massive educational complex to join with the military, industry, and health care sector as essential large-scale modern institutions.

The University of Kentucky, as a land grant school, was especially well placed to reap a rich harvest from these postwar changes. One such development, with broad ramifications for later, came in 1948 when UK opened its Northern Extension Center in Covington, Kentucky, just across the Ohio River from Cincinnati. The Extension Center represented an effort by UK to reach out in some tangible way to the local community to provide academic and technical courses and programs, and perhaps later even certificate or degree programs.

Creation of the Northern Extension Center was a more natural gesture for UK than might be recognized at first. In fact, since 1919, the University served as the accreditation "agency" for Kentucky junior and community colleges. Usually such duties are the function of regional accreditation associations, various ones being scattered about the country. However, no such organization accredited Kentucky junior and community colleges until 1923, according to the Larry Stanley study of Kentucky community colleges, when the Southern Association of Colleges and Schools, or SACS, began to do so on a limited basis. Even so, until 1952, UK continued to oversee and accredit Kentucky junior and community college programs.

So a long and intimate relationship existed early on between the University of Kentucky and the Kentucky junior and community colleges, well before UK formally gained administrative oversight of the state comprehensive community college system, long before the Covington Northern Extension Center opened. Since 1919, UK had cultivated statewide relationships through these schools, and now it began to create such schools of its own. This network of campuses gave the University tremendous influence from Ashland to Paducah and beyond. It greatly enhanced the state university's political power, both in the communities directly affected and ultimately in Kentucky's capital city, Frankfort.

Another clear measure of gain came with the development of the University's new Albert Benjamin Chandler Medical Center, named after Kentucky's gregarious singing governor, nicknamed "Happy," a former U.S. senator and baseball commissioner. Ground was broken for the UK Chandler Medical Center in 1956, and in 1960 matriculated its first medical school students. UK's Medical Center will play a crucial role in the development of the University of Kentucky's community college in Lexington, and would wield tremendous influence in the creation of its health care-related programs, in addition to its influence upon health care-related programs statewide.

▲ Lexington Technical Institute nursing class of 1968. First row, left to right: Evelyn Skaggs, Dixie Cox, Carolyn Waggoner, Susan Schneidor; second row: Molly McWilliams, Cathy Casey, Anita Shout, Donna McKnight, Penny Daffin, Gayle Laranert; third row: Kathy McCarthy, Barb Cooper, Roxie Potts, Beth Speaks, Karen Hareld, Donna Overmyer. Not pictured: Karen Ritchie. Photograph and names provided courtesy of Donna Overmyer.

UK's Agricultural Extension Service, created in 1910 as one of America's first such services, also provided the University with greater statewide clout. And just as the Agricultural Extension Service was a national model for other such organizations, it was a model or template for extended rural health care services in the early 1960s via Dr. Kurt Deuschle's groundbreaking community medicine program at UK. By the time the state community colleges joined UK, the University's presence in Kentucky seemed virtually ubiquitous.

Students of the University of Kentucky and of this period in Kentucky higher education have styled the 1950s advancement of the extension centers as highly significant; one called it the "most significant development in the two-year college movement" in Kentucky. Vital to this growth was UK President Frank G. Dickey. Only thirty-eight years old when he took hold of the UK helm, Dickey understood and certainly appreciated the many advantages to be garnered by these extension centers. He could foresee additional centers, even if he perhaps did not see them for what they were: the foundation of the University of Kentucky Community College System.

Not only was UK expanding, but so too was Lexington, finally emerging from years of what might be termed a somewhat sluggish growth pattern. After great initial promise in the late eighteenth and early nineteenth centuries, Lexington found itself faced with a truly serious constraint to growth imposed by geography: no river. Town Branch of Elkhorn Creek meanders through the town center, but the nearest river is the Kentucky, some twenty-five miles to the south. By the 1950s, though, technological advances allowed for additional expansion, and just in time. A great influx of new physicians, dentists, nurses, behavioral and natural scientists, and other support staff poured into Lexington to work at the UK Medical Center. There also came a fresh business partner for the community with the arrival of a major new typewriter-manufacturing facility owned by International Business Machines, Inc., i.e., IBM, the "other" Big Blue. Between them, the Medical Center and IBM brought many new residents

▲ Peter P. Bosomworth, M.D., of the Albert B. Chandler Medical Center of the University of Kentucky, later that institution's chancellor, played an important role in helping several Lexington Technical Institute programs. 2001UA028:5288, University of Kentucky Archives

Kentucky became one of only four states, ...where the major state university governed the state-sponsored community colleges.

to central Kentucky, a good many of them upstate New Yorkers, an infusion of "new blood" injected into the previously rather stagnant, stodgy, blue-blood–minded horse capital of the world that many felt to be beneficial, welcome, and long overdue.

Another benefit came in the personage of Bert T. Combs, who occupied the strategically critical position of state governor. Deeply rooted in southern and eastern Kentucky heritage, Combs was a progressive Democratic governor as well as a brilliant jurist, and a true and staunch supporter of Kentucky's educational system from top to bottom, all features pointed out by Pulitzer prize–winning journalist John Ed Pearce. During his administration, from 1959 to 1963, Kentucky saw implemented the merit system for hiring state government employees, the formation of Kentucky's Human Rights

▲ Richard P. Moloney, Sr.

Commission, the beginning of Kentucky's educational television network KET, new roads and highways constructed, and desegregation of Kentucky public accommodations. UK's Medical Center blossomed under his watch. "Chandler took the lead role and the political risk, with the help of Dr. William R. Willard. He got the legislative support and the initial funding and ultimately the recognition" for the Medical Center, remembered UK Medical Center Chancellor Peter P. Bosomworth, M.D., in an interview. Chandler's successor, Governor Bert Combs, continued Bosomworth, brought in a lot of money for the Medical Center afterwards to make sure it continued to run.

Another Combs accomplishment came through the spawning of the Kentucky comprehensive community college system, and its placement under the direction of the University of Kentucky. Indispensable assistance and political backing for this measure came from state representative Richard P. Moloney, Sr., the Democratic majority leader. With his ducks in a row, Combs on January 2, 1962, addressed the

General Assembly; there he proposed generation of a state-sponsored comprehensive community college network. This "marked a definite change in the nature of junior colleges" and community colleges, Pearce noted. Beforehand, the schools were created under a wide range of circumstances. Now, "Combs made them a unified system, with uniform requirements and standards, fees, and tuition. And he placed them under the University of Kentucky, which had the power to enforce performance standards and to recommend new community colleges."

Objections came from the regional colleges and universities—they wanted either direct control over the community college in their immediate vicinity or a completely separate, independent board to oversee all of the community colleges—but the plan nevertheless went forward. Kentucky became one of only four states, including Alaska, Hawaii, and Pennsylvania, where the major state university governed the state-sponsored community colleges, according to Cohen and Brawer. Those Kentucky communities directly affected by the new system seemed generally pleased with the arrangement.

But Lexington did not yet fit into the new community college mix. Tremendous growth in central Kentucky certainly seemed to recommend a community college for Lexington, or at least some sort of institution that would accommodate programs traditionally offered by a community college. Demand seemed only to increase for support-level personnel, semiprofessionals, and technicians to accommodate the UK Medical Center and IBM. Also, longer established health care concerns in Lexington likewise experienced growth and subsequent shortages of personnel, such as the Lexington Clinic and the major hospitals—Central Baptist, Good Samaritan, and St. Joseph—as Lexington solidified its position as a regional medical center for central and eastern Kentucky.

With the health care industry experiencing such rapid growth, two areas presented dire shortages in need of immediate redress. Far too few nurses were available, a shortage that was not only local but also national in scope. Another need presented itself with the 1962 opening of the University of Kentucky College of Dentistry, now in want of dental laboratory technicians and their skills for making crowns, dentures, and other such "prosthetic appliances."

More and more nurses received their training from colleges and universities rather than through the old method of hospital nursing school training. Two- and four-year nursing programs appeared with increased frequency in community colleges and universities, respectively. Dental laboratory technicians only recently had formed college-level programs. One of the earliest models was the program at Southern Illinois University in Carbondale, but it was not popular at first with the larger dental care community dominated by dentists, who saw this development as a possible threat to their prerogatives and authority. Nevertheless, calls went up for UK to provide such a program, and ultimately just such a program would be provided in Lexington.

A brief delay met creation of these and other programs when UK President Dickey resigned in 1963 to become director of the Southern Association of Colleges and Schools. Dickey would leave to his successor the task of forming the structure of the University with its added community colleges. Fortunately, the incoming president was well equipped to meet the organizational challenge.

John W. Oswald, Ph.D., was executive vice president of the University of California when he came to UK, and as such was quite familiar with the difficulties and responsibilities inherent to a multicampus institution. With the help of interim president A. D. Albright, graduate dean A. D. Kirwan, and longtime history professor Thomas D. Clark, Oswald would become the change agent the University required, a man who believed "the way that the University of Kentucky could grow as an institution was on its academic merits."

▲ John W. Oswald, Ph.D., president of the University of Kentucky. 2001UA028:3363, University of Kentucky Archives

In a 1987 interview with UK's Terry Birdwhistell, Jack Oswald recalled the rather seductive recruitment process he experienced in Lexington, filled with Kentucky-style charm. Interesting to Oswald, too, was the attitude he found from UK board members and faculty for moving the University beyond its more "provincial" status as a "strictly southern university" toward attaining "greater stature." In fact, changes already were "on the drawing board" of UK faculty themselves, including calls for a stronger faculty, better retirement plans, and higher salary schedules. For the most part, Oswald agreed with these plans.

John W. Oswald ...would become the change agent the University required...

In the end, the sales pitch must have been really good, for Oswald and his wife Rose accepted the Kentucky assignment, leaving behind a job at what arguably was the best state university system in the country, with a home in Berkeley that claimed a coveted view of San Francisco's Golden Gate Bridge, among other perks.

Oswald found "particularly intriguing" the new state community college system proposed by outgoing governor Combs and supported by incoming governor Edward T. "Ned" Breathitt. Oswald enjoyed the challenges and responsibilities posed by oversight of a multicampus institution in California, and welcomed similar duties in Kentucky. In fact, expansion of the system already occupied his mind; Oswald asked, for example, if Louisville was "out of bounds," since he believed a UK community college should be there. "Any great or first-rate university in this state must have a...strong base and tie in the largest metropolitan area of the state," he said, and a community college would provide such a base. Oswald knew also that UK needed a stronger tie into the local Lexington and central Kentucky community, such as provided by a community college or a reasonable variation on its theme.

Overall, Oswald conceived of a two-tiered organizational scheme within the University of Kentucky to accommodate the addition of the community colleges. His idea was various units of the Lexington campus would fall under the direction of the University System, while a Community College System would organize those far-flung units of the University. Developed and proposed by Dr. Oswald, in January 1964, the UK Board of Trustees approved of the two systems, both ultimately under the administrative direction of the UK Board of Trustees and the President of the University, per the Stanley study. Discussion then ensued to allow for a technical institute on UK's central campus, and an emergency budget was recommended for the first biennium (i.e., July 1, 1964 to June 30, 1966), and approved of in January 1965 by the UK Board. With these actions, a major hurdle had been cleared, and a firm foundation was now in place from which to push the University and its community colleges forward.

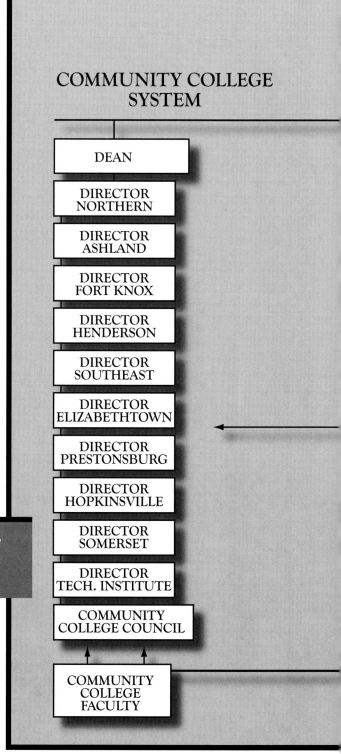

Organizational flow chart from the "University of Kentucky Bulletin: Community College System, 1966–1967" shows the two-tiered University and Community College System organizational scheme created by President Oswald.

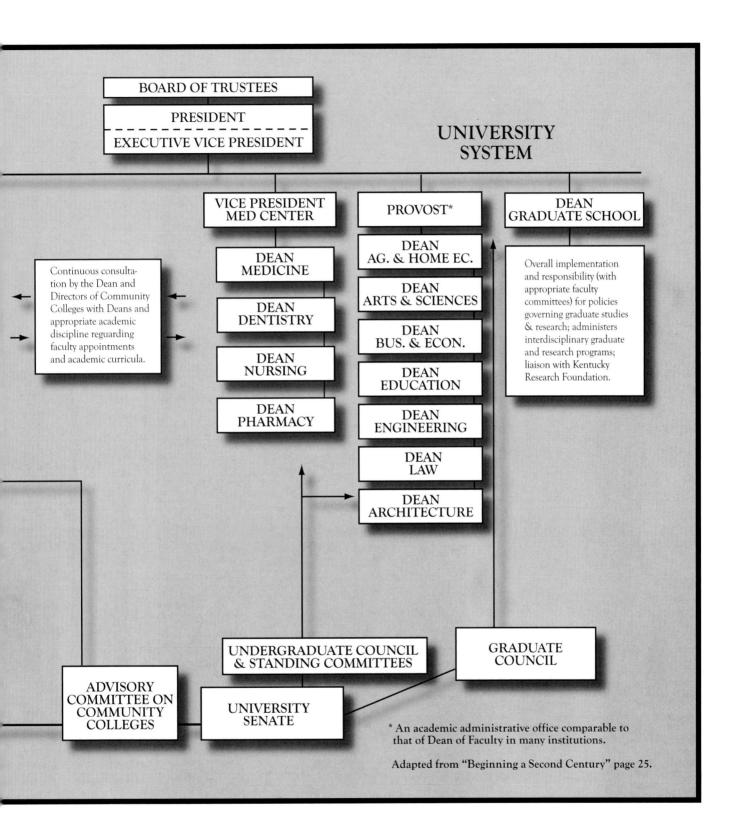

BOARD OF TRUSTEES

PRESIDENT
- - - - - - - - - - - - - - - -
EXECUTIVE VICE PRESIDENT

UNIVERSITY SYSTEM

VICE PRESIDENT MED CENTER

PROVOST*

DEAN GRADUATE SCHOOL

Continuous consultation by the Dean and Directors of Community Colleges with Deans and appropriate academic discipline reguarding faculty appointments and academic curricula.

DEAN MEDICINE

DEAN DENTISTRY

DEAN NURSING

DEAN PHARMACY

DEAN AG. & HOME EC.

DEAN ARTS & SCIENCES

DEAN BUS. & ECON.

DEAN EDUCATION

DEAN ENGINEERING

DEAN LAW

DEAN ARCHITECTURE

Overall implementation and responsibility (with appropriate faculty committees) for policies governing graduate studies & research; administers interdisciplinary graduate and research programs; liaison with Kentucky Research Foundation.

UNDERGRADUATE COUNCIL & STANDING COMMITTEES

GRADUATE COUNCIL

ADVISORY COMMITTEE ON COMMUNITY COLLEGES

UNIVERSITY SENATE

* An academic administrative office comparable to that of Dean of Faculty in many institutions.

Adapted from "Beginning a Second Century" page 25.

◀ Breckinridge Hall, located on the west side of the quadrangle on the corner of Rose Street and Washington Avenue, was originally constructed as a University of Kentucky dormitory. Opened in 1930, Breckinridge hosted some of the first administrative offices for Lexington Technical Institute.

▼ Frazee Hall on the University of Kentucky campus hosted the first offices of the Lexington Technical Institute. Originally home of the Department and then College of Education, Frazee opened in 1907 and was renamed in 1931 after D. F. Frazee, a former UK Board of Trustees member. Photo courtesy of UK Public Relations and Marketing.

When the Lexington Technical Institute (LTI) began operations in 1965 as the Lexington version of a community college at UK, it had a mere twenty students in its keeping and only two programs, one leading to the associate degree in Nursing and the other an associate degree in Dental Laboratory Technology. Major funding to start these two programs came through grants from the W. K. Kellogg Fund, one of the world's largest philanthropies, created in 1930 by the founder of Kellogg breakfast cereals. Authorized by the UK Board of Trustees in January 1965, the program started on a shoestring, with administrative work housed where there was room, including Frazee Hall on main campus facing South Limestone Street, and in a former residence on the northeast corner of Rose Street and Euclid Avenue. In 1972, LTI administration moved on to the more "stately" digs of the third floor of Breckinridge Hall, part of the quadrangle of buildings on the corner of Rose and Washington on UK's main campus.

LTI students applied for admission to the Institute, and afterward were eligible for virtually all of the amenities of University life, according to the January 1968 LTI catalog and bulletin, except for membership in the social fraternities and sororities. Full-time students, i.e., those registered for at least twelve semester hours, were eligible to attend sporting and cultural events, and had access to the University Health Service. Student fees for LTI students would be the same as those attending UK. Financial aid could be sought through the UK Student Financial Aid Office, and LTI students could apply for University housing. Course work would be through

the specific program assigned, with general education courses taken through the University.

Pat McDermott presented a unique view of the early days of Lexington Technical Institute development in an interview. A Paris, Kentucky, native, McDermott responded to his father's query on what he wanted to do when he graduated from high school by saying he wanted to attend college. McDermott was among the many young Americans of the day who wanted to avoid a military tour in Vietnam. A college deferment would do the trick, but McDermott had no idea what it was he wanted to do. McDermott's father later took a trip to see the family dentist, Jim Shipp. Shipp asked about the younger man, and the father told of his dilemma on what to study. Shipp suggested a new dental laboratory program at UK. He called Dr. Ross Stromberg, a professor of prosthodontics at the UK Dental School who, along with John Kemper, a dental laboratory technology graduate of the program at Southern Illinois University at Carbondale, was starting a new dental lab program at UK under its new LTI unit. "Nobody knew what LTI meant, or where it was," recalled McDermott. In July 1965, seventeen-year-old McDermott talked with the "crusty" Dr. Stromberg, a Florida native, in his office on the fifth floor of the teaching laboratory of the dental laboratory technology program, room D-530. Stromberg sent McDermott to visit a working dental lab in town to see the actual conditions under which the work was done. Fascinated by what he saw, McDermott was ready to try his hand at dental lab technology, and was brought in with the very first class of students in the program, one of only five such programs in the country.

To enter the dental laboratory technology program, students were required to take the ACT (American College Testing program, started in 1959), a standardized achievement test for college admission preferred by most southern and midwestern colleges and universities over the SAT (originally the Scholastic Aptitude Test, started in 1926), favored on the east and west coasts. A minimum score of seventeen was required, and McDermott made the grade. "They also gave the carving portion of the dental aptitude test," according to McDermott, the same taken by dental college students, "at that time about two cylinders about six inches long and about two inches in diameter of a green chalk. They gave you a straight-edged knife and instructions, and you had to make cuts to certain dimensions and at certain angles. And then the faculty would grade these, evaluate them, for accuracy…. The grading went from a minus one through zero to a plus nine." McDermott made the grade to enter the nine-member first class, in a program that would become only more and more competitive over time, certainly one of the best of its kind in the United States. For McDermott, it was the opportunity of a lifetime: he went on not only to practice his art, but also to teach it at LTI.

A grant from the Kellogg Foundation got the program started. The UK program was unique, according to McDermott, because it was the only one established within the actual physical confines of a dental school. This, he recalled, was a great advantage to UK dental lab students because they often were instructed by actual dental college faculty. UK's College of Dentistry was one of the newest in America at that time, so everything was state-of-the-art, and the faculty was top flight, so the dental lab students were being exposed to the best. It was a good environment.

Key in establishing the nursing program at LTI was Marie L. Piekarski. Piekarski had trained as a nurse in New Jersey and at the University of Pennsylvania. She had a long-established career behind her when she was recruited to come to Lexington to set up an associate degree program in nursing. She met with several University personnel, including the University's executive vice president, Dr. A. D. Albright, who, over the course of a long career, became a great leader in Kentucky education and politics, and Dr. Marcia Dake,

▲ John Fuhrmann and Pat McDermott, Dental Lab graduates and former LCC instructors, own Fuhrmann & McDermott Dental Laboratories in Lexington, Kentucky.

the first dean of the UK College of Nursing. Piekarski was wooed away from her job in Florida to take on the somewhat daunting and exciting task of building a program from scratch. She did all the original planning for the nursing program, recruited the original nursing faculty, and actually participated in interviewing the first class of nursing students to enter the program in her offices in Frazee Hall. Piekarski remembered that one prospective student was fifty-nine years old; when asked why she wanted in the nursing program with all its rigors and demands, she responded that she had always wanted to be a registered nurse, and she saw this program as her chance. She and a few other nontraditional students would form the first class of LTI nursing students.

Nursing students attended their regular course lectures, such as chemistry and anatomy and physiology, in classrooms assigned to the LTI college, such as the nursing laboratory in the basement of the Funkhouser building, as one former LTI administration member recalled. Clinical training came through associations with the various and relatively numerous hospitals, clinics, and local health care agencies in the Lexington area. Students in the two-year program were required to receive at least a "C" grade in all nursing courses. Successful completion of the program resulted in the Associate in Applied Science degree, and graduates were then qualified to take the state licensing examination to become registered nurses.

For Dental Laboratory Technology, students would be under the direct supervision of the UK College of Dentistry for all instruction and curricular matters. LTI administered the program. Among other things, students in this program would study dental anatomy, occlusion, fixed prosthodontics, and maxillofacial prosthesis, in addition to such general education courses as physics, chemistry, and psychology. In fact, much of the training parallels that of dental students, at least in certain phases of technical skills instruction, so designed to result in clear communication between dentist and technician. Two years of training found reward in the Associate in Applied Science degree and subsequent technical work in a dental office or dental laboratory.

It did not take long for LTI to grow, both in student body and in program offerings. From the original 20 students in 1965, the number jumped to 174 by 1968, with an additional eight associate degree programs added by that same year. Now students could study to record brain waves in the electroencephalography technology program, with the UK neurology department and other clinical and LTI faculty direction; enter a twenty-eight-month radiologic technology program that emphasized diagnostic radiograph production, optimal radiation therapy, and procedures using radioisotopes, with much of the direction coming from the UK University Hospital radiology department faculty; or study to become a respiratory therapist under the direction of the anesthesiology department of the UK Medical Center.

One graduate of the respiratory care program, Francis "Tri" Roberts, remembered well the important

> *It did not take long for LTI to grow, both in student body and in program offerings. From the original 20 students in 1965, the number jumped to 174 by 1968, with an additional eight associate degree programs added by that same year.*

contribution of the UK Medical Center in helping create this and other programs in the Institute. Roberts recalled the "critical" role played by Dr. Peter P. Bosomworth, a young anesthesiologist who later became chancellor of the UK Medical Center, in establishing respiratory care. Marie Piekarski remembered those especially important advocates in the medical center for other such programmatic developments, who included Bosomworth; Dr. William R. Willard, first dean of medicine and vice president of the UK Medical Center, and as founding father of the family practice field as a specialty, a true pioneer in medical education in the United States; Dr. Joseph Hamburg, dean of Allied Health Professions; Dr. Al Morris, dean of the College of Dentistry and later University vice president; and Mr. Robert Johnson, a public and political relations specialist who later served as a UK vice president, vice president of the University of California at Berkeley, and also as president of Appalachian Regional Healthcare, Inc.

LTI decided to look into other disciplines and began to offer programs in such non-medical or non-health care related areas as a civil engineering technology cooperative program, including a year of course work and a year of field work in direct contact with scientists and engineers; electrical and mechanical engineering technologies, designed to enhance the background of individuals already engaged in related fields; professional secretaryship, with specializations in general, medical, or legal secretarial work offered; and the first year in a Forestry and Wood Technology program, with the second year held in residence at the Wood Utilization Center in Quicksand, a hamlet in Breathitt County named for Quicksand Creek, about a mile and a half southeast of Jackson, Kentucky.

Administratively, the Community College System was organized with a vice president at its head, who also acted as dean, Dr. Ellis Hartford. Hartford would report to Dr. Albright, who reported to President Oswald. More specific to the Institute, the man first charged with actual oversight of the LTI operation was Dr. Edsel

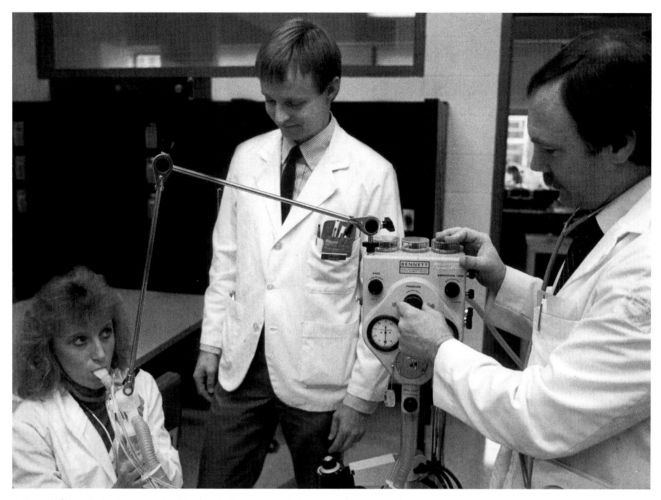

▲ A youthful Tri Roberts, center, tending his duties as a Respiratory Care faculty member.

Godbey, assistant dean of the UK Community College System. A native of Casey County, Kentucky, Godbey came to UK in 1957. As one might expect, he had solid credentials and background for such a post as director of a community college. He served as director of the Southeast Community College at Cumberland for three years before returning to Lexington, where he was assigned to the Extended Programs office with "special responsibility" to develop the new community colleges. Godbey was granted a one-year leave-of-absence in 1966 to serve as director of the College Preparatory Center Program for SACS, according to the UK school newspaper, the *Kentucky Kernel*, of March 11, 1966.

Godbey's tenure was short, and his departure provided for his replacement by Dr. Charles T. Wethington, Jr. Another Casey County native, Wethington was appointed to serve a one-year stint as acting director of LTI. Once again, the chosen director held extensive aca-

demic credentials and a broad educational background and experience. Wethington joined the University in 1965 as an instructor of Educational Psychology before taking on the LTI assignment. His own academic background was interesting: two years at Brescia College, a coeducational Roman Catholic institution founded in Owensboro, Kentucky, in 1950 by the Ursuline Sisters of Mount Saint Joseph. From there he moved on to Eastern Kentucky University (EKU) in Richmond, and in 1956 graduated with a Bachelor of Arts in history and English. In 1958–59, Wethington studied at the Russian Center of Syracuse University as part of his 1957 through 1961 assignment in the United States Air Force Security Service as a cryptolinguist. He had teaching experience in Liberty High School in Casey County, the San Juan, California, school system, and as an Air Force instructor in Japan. Wethington received his Master of Arts (1962) and Doctor of Philosophy in Education (1966) degrees from the University of

◀ Dr. Edsel Godbey, first director of Lexington Technical Institute. 2001UA028:1672, University of Kentucky Archives

▼ Dr. Charles T. Wethington, Jr., second director of Lexington Technical Institute. 2001UA028:5701, University of Kentucky Archives

◀ M. L. Archer, fourth director of Lexington Technical Institute. 2001UA028:0120, University of Kentucky Archives

▼ G. Robert Boyd, Ph.D., third director of Lexington Technical Institute. 2001UA028:0412, University of Kentucky Archives

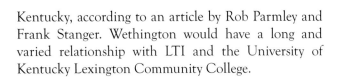

Kentucky, according to an article by Rob Parmley and Frank Stanger. Wethington would have a long and varied relationship with LTI and the University of Kentucky Lexington Community College.

In 1967, Wethington moved to Maysville, on the Ohio River in Mason County, Kentucky, as director of Maysville Community College. Then, in 1971, he became assistant vice president for the Community College System, and in 1981, vice president of the Community College System. In 1982, the University reorganized its administrative structure and Wethington received the title of chancellor of the Community College System. As vice president and chancellor, Wethington oversaw many changes to the Kentucky community colleges under UK's charge, including the addition of many new programs and many more new students. According to Parmley and Stanger, he would continue to have a close relationship with the community colleges well into and beyond his years served as president of the University of Kentucky.

G. Robert Boyd replaced Dr. Wethington as LTI director in 1967. Boyd was a graduate of Western Kentucky University in Bowling Green, and held M.A. and Ph.D. degrees from UK. The requisite academic background complemented years of experience in secondary and postsecondary education. Prior to becoming director of LTI, Boyd was a teacher in the Kentucky high school system and served for twenty years as a dean at Troy State University in Alabama. Dr. Boyd wanted to spread the word about Lexington Technical Institute. In an October 31, 1967, UK

press release, Boyd explained that LTI programs were intended "to prepare the student for immediate employment on a technical or semi-professional level." Two years later, in a March 6, 1969, University press release, Boyd was quoted saying, "We never discourage a student from pursuing a four-year college degree, but if he is interested in a two-year associate degree we are interested in him.... We know many students do not have the time or the means to attend college for four years, so we believe that our type of training is an idea whose time has come." Seeming to bear out Boyd's observations was the headcount at LTI. During the two years from 1967 to 1969, the student body numbers doubled, from 112 to 232. Since the Institute opened in 1965 with only two programs, LTI now offered fifteen different paths of study.

While Boyd looked after the LTI programs, turmoil dominated the University president's office. Dr. Oswald found himself embroiled in controversy, including political fights with the powers that be in the state capital in Frankfort. Between various challenges to his authority and even academic freedom issues, Oswald resigned his position in 1968. For a year, UK legend Albert D. "Ab" Kirwan served as interim president. Kirwan, a UK letterman in football and track, then head football coach from 1938 to 1945, then dean of men, dean of students, and later dean of the Graduate School, also became a history professor at the University. Kirwan brought stability to campus and helped smooth the way for Dr. Otis A. Singletary in 1969, according to a Frank Stanger biographical sketch on the UK president.

For LTI, the troubles faced at the top of the administration on main campus did not impede progress. Actually, the path toward one important milestone began in 1969 when the Institute completed its first self-study and entertained a visit that November from a committee representing the Southern Association of Colleges and Schools. Accreditation, so important a force in education, so critical in granting confirmation of curriculum and methodological credibility, came in December 1971 for LTI. SACS accreditation gave the Institute programs the sort of national recognition desired by all institutions of higher learning, and gave confidence to the students in those programs that they were receiving proper training and earning degrees of value at LTI.

Boyd's tenure as LTI director was nearly as short as that of his predecessors; in 1969, Maurice Lee Archer, or M. L., began a one-year posting as acting director. Born in Jellico, Tennessee, Archer held a B.S. degree from the University of Tennessee and an M.A. from the University of Kentucky. Archer, like Godbey before him, had high school teaching experience, Archer's in the Scott County schools, as well as the Elliott County school system. Apparently pleased with his performance in the temporary acting director role, in 1970 UK officials appointed Archer LTI director. Continuing the tradition established before his arrival, he oversaw continued expansion and development. Programs grew, and so did the ranks of faculty to teach in them. By 1972, LTI had a full-time faculty of twenty and thirty more part-time. General education courses for the LTI student body continued to be taught by University faculty. New programs continued to enter the curriculum, such as recreation leadership, data processing, transportation, social work, and vocational teaching. Nursing and Dental Laboratory Technology continued to thrive. According to Archer, business careers attracted the most students, followed by nursing and allied health programs. Archer reported with pride in the *Lexington Herald-Leader* that the entire 1971 graduating class of nurses passed the state board examination.

"We believe that our type of training is an idea whose time has come."

A new program in real estate got underway in 1972, a two-year program leading to an associate degree in that booming field. For the convenience of those already engaged in real estate, either as students or instructors, courses were held at night for both beginners and experienced agents. Just as was the case in other programs, the real estate associate's required not only a strong concentration in the field itself, but also the broadening of the mind in other fields of endeavor, such as English, sociology, psychology, and mathematics, in addition to a minimum number of elective courses. According to a University press release that quoted Archer, real estate students could expect preparation for additional training in "land development, commercial property management, finance, real estate marketing and farm brokerage, in addition to becoming a real estate licensee."

New programs continued to come through the early 1970s, just as the Institute continued to grow. When Archer was about to retire in 1973 as director of LTI, the headcount for the Institute rang up at 1,118 students. Important programs added to the cast included the Architectural Technology program that would prepare students for careers in architectural design, with a building technology option. Beginning in the 1971–72 academic year, architectural technology students would work with architects and engineers as part of their training. Architectural graphics, blueprint reading, freehand drawing and model construction, construction documents and reproductions, and technical communications were offered alongside the theory and history of architecture, surveying, and college algebra and trigonometry, according to the *UK Community College System Bulletin*, vol. 63, no. 2, February 1971.

In seeming leaps and bounds, Lexington Technical Institute was fulfilling its mission to bring a broader range of training options to the greater Lexington and central Kentucky region. Its growth served as an apparent confirmation that the need for the Institute and its programs was large already and growing still. There was no reason to think the future would be otherwise.

2
Growing with the Times

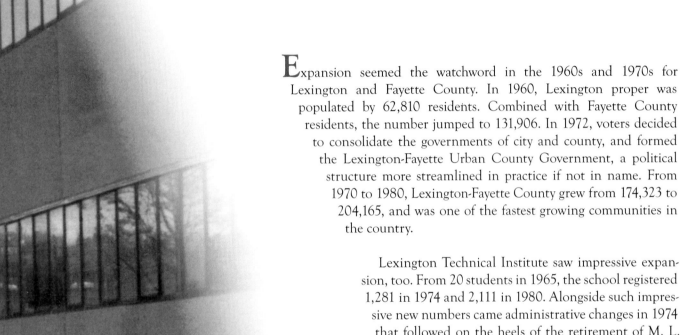

Expansion seemed the watchword in the 1960s and 1970s for Lexington and Fayette County. In 1960, Lexington proper was populated by 62,810 residents. Combined with Fayette County residents, the number jumped to 131,906. In 1972, voters decided to consolidate the governments of city and county, and formed the Lexington-Fayette Urban County Government, a political structure more streamlined in practice if not in name. From 1970 to 1980, Lexington-Fayette County grew from 174,323 to 204,165, and was one of the fastest growing communities in the country.

Lexington Technical Institute saw impressive expansion, too. From 20 students in 1965, the school registered 1,281 in 1974 and 2,111 in 1980. Alongside such impressive new numbers came administrative changes in 1974 that followed on the heels of the retirement of M. L. Archer. New to the College helm was Dr. William N. Price, a New Hampshire native with B.S., M.A., and Ed.D. degrees, all from Arizona State University in Tempe. Price seemed to have an appropriate background for the directorship. Before becoming LTI director, Price was associate director of Henderson Community College, a lovely campus located a few miles west of Owensboro, Kentucky, and Evansville, Indiana, all three communities banked on the Ohio River. Price could claim the proud distinction of military service, ranked a major in the United States Marine Corps Reserve. Over the next several years, Price would lead the school on its mission of community service, putting his own unique stamp on the administration of Lexington Technical Institute.

◀ Oswald Building, Lexington Technical Institute, shortly after opening in 1976.

New programs appeared in the 1970s, designed to address community needs broadly defined on a geographic level and to meet the service component of the Institute's overall mission. For example, programs that entered the LTI curriculum at this juncture included Fire Science Technology, Manufacturing Technology, Nuclear Medicine Technology, and Recreation Leadership. According to the 1975–76 *UK Community College System Bulletin*, Fire Science prepared graduates for job opportunities in the insurance industry, inspection agencies, fire protection equipment manufacturers, and with fire companies, with the added goal in training leaders in community fire prevention. Manufacturing Technology was geared toward industry, and offered training in various manufacturing processes and techniques, aimed toward preparation for an industrial plant supervisor. Nuclear Medicine Technology training enabled its practitioners to perform diagnostic and therapeutic procedures using sundry radioactive materials. Recreation Leadership prepared students for work in local, state, and federal parks, camps, youth organizations, recreation departments, hospitals, and correctional institutions, where they could plan and direct recreational activities for participants, patients, or inhabitants, dependent upon institutional function.

In the *Lexington Technical Institute Annual Report* for July 1, 1977, to June 30, 1978, it was reported that "Associate Health Technologies enrollment has remained at the maximum fixed enrollment levels, and the first students were admitted to the new Dental Hygiene Program. All Business Technology and Engineering Technology Programs have shared in the growth, except for the Fire Science Program. Participation in the Co-Op program has increased from 187 to 210 student placements.... Special English and Mathematics courses serving a total of over 400 students were established for under-prepared students and integrated with the existing Study Skills Program. Plans for an expanded Developmental Program for 1978–79 are being formalized. Library circulation activities increased 44 percent and 784 items were added to our collection.... A total of 234 people graduated from LTI in May 1978. Of this number, 194 are employed in a job related to their major, 14 are working in an unrelated job, five are planning to continue their education and 20 are unemployed (12 of these are not seeking employment)." These words were seconded, essentially verbatim, by LTI associate director F. David Wilkin in the same report. It was a positive document that registered substantial strides forward for the Institute.

▲ William N. Price, Ed.D., fifth director of Lexington Technical Institute. 2001UA028:3627, University of Kentucky Archives

When it came to class location, LTI classes might meet just about anywhere on UK's campus during the 1960s to the mid-1970s. No doubt scheduling often proved a real challenge to those charged with coordinating University space. Over the whole range of the UK campus one could find LTI classes meeting, from the Old Agricultural Building to McVey and Kastle Halls, to the Commerce Building and Pence and Anderson Halls, on to the Chemistry-Physics (Chem-Phys) Building, Bowman Hall, White Hall, Erickson, and Funkhouser. Chances were favorable that one would get to know UK's main campus rather well over the course of an LTI program.

LTI students, especially those many students enrolled in health care–related programs, also utilized off-campus facilities. Dental clinics, for example, were held in the Veterans Administration (VA) Hospital, Eastern State Hospital, Cardinal Hill Hospital, and the UK Medical Center. For nursing students, training took place at Good Samaritan, Central Baptist, St. Joseph, and Shriners hospitals, the Child Development Center, and the UK, VA, and Cardinal Hill facilities. Respiratory care students trained in various departments of the UK, VA, Central Baptist, and St. Joseph

A Brief History of the Nuclear Medicine Technology Program at LTI/LCC

The Nuclear Medicine Technology (NMT) program at Lexington Technical Institute (LTI) originated in the early 1970s at the Veterans Administration Hospital (VAH) and the University of Kentucky Medical Center (UKMC) to train technologists separately from the x-ray technology students. A national movement of NMT education and certification examination had begun in the 1960s. From the early days of the Radioisotope Lab until the specialty of Nuclear Medicine was recognized, nuclear medicine technologists had come from the ranks of x-ray technologists.

In 1973, Robert Beihn, a research radiation biologist at VAH, began to teach NMT to LTI students. In addition Guy Simmons, PhD, a VA radiation physicist, and a radiopharmacist, John Coupal, PhD, provided classroom instruction in the VAH Nuclear Medicine department. Clinical instruction for patient procedures was provided both at VAMC and UKMC. The *Compendium of Selected Data & Characteristics (1975-1976)* published by the University of Kentucky Community College System states that there were five AAS degrees awarded in 1975 to students in NMT.

In 1978, an early program graduate, Michael Huffaker, who worked briefly for Beihn in his research, was approached to apply for the coordinator's job. He was hired by LTI as the first NMT program coordinator.

From 1978 to 1982, the program was on shaky financial ground, and in 1980 lost VA funding. The University declined to be the program sponsor. As a result, the program was deactivated on June 30, 1980, for one year. Eastern Kentucky University was approached in regards to relocating the program since funding was not forthcoming from the University. UKMC gave funding for the 1982-1983 academic year, and in May 1982, an agreement was reached between Dr Charles Wethington, Chancellor of the UK Community College System, and Dr William Price, Director, LTI, that as of July 1983, the NMT program would be funded by the Community College System as a 12-month, advance standing program. Mike Huffaker remained as program coordinator through most of 1982, and he is to be credited with pursuing and establishing the financial stability of the program. In addition to this, Mike worked to initiate the external programmatic accreditation which was eventually granted in April 1983 after he had left as program coordinator.

Scott R. Sechrist was hired as the second coordinator in January 1983. He had trained at the University of North Carolina at Chapel Hill and had been both staff technologist and chief technologist at Norfolk General Hospital, Norfolk, Virginia. In addition to completing the accreditation process, Sechrist began to reorganize the curriculum of the program. The new curriculum was one year of general education and one year of technical courses. He left the program at the end of the summer term 1987 to begin a baccalaureate NMT program at Old Dominion University in Norfolk.

The third, and current, program coordinator, Charles H. Coulston, was hired to begin in September 1987. He is a graduate of the NMT program at Indiana University – Purdue University at Indianapolis, Indiana. He had worked at Good Samaritan Hospital in Lexington for 5 years. Since 1987, the program has increased its clinical affiliation with local institutions, and the curriculum has been revised to integrate the technical courses throughout the 22 months of the program. Currently the program has a 5-year average (2001-2006) pass rate of 91% which is equal to the national average.

Charles H. Coulston

A Brief History of the Nuclear Medicine Technology Program, by Professor Charles Coulston.

hospitals. Engineering Technology utilized the machine shop at Central Kentucky State Vocational Technical School. According to the 1980 *LTI Self-Study*, off-campus courses also were offered at IBM and at the Federal Correctional Institute (FCI), both located in Fayette County.

Dispersed as they were to so many different venues, many LTI faculty, staff, and students hoped that someday they could have a single facility for most of their course work, although it was understood that of necessity much clinical work would continue off campus. Interestingly, despite a presence all over the UK main campus, many, probably most, UK students and faculty knew absolutely nothing about LTI; in fact, most probably did not know it existed, even after years of operation. Thus it seemed that one sure sign that the Institute was moving toward better defining itself came when the University decided to construct a building exclusively dedicated to LTI programs and personnel. Ground was broken in 1974 on a site that once had been nothing more than a great pasture field, across from the new UK football field at Commonwealth Stadium. Apparently what recommended the site to University and Kentucky state officials, according to Marie Piekarski, was proximity to the UK campus, especially the UK Medical Center, readily available parking, and the availability of the space itself.

While virtually all those tied to LTI welcomed the opening in 1976 of the new John W. Oswald Building, others viewed this momentous event as the actual date that marked when LTI "really" got started as a distinct institution. One hundred and twenty thousand square feet of fresh space thus appeared in August 1976, year of the nation's bicentennial, named for the UK president who was so important in the history and even the creation of the UK Community College System, and specifically the history and creation of Lexington Technical Institute. Now all LTI programs, faculty, staff, and administrative offices could be housed under one roof, a building all could associate exclusively with the Institute and its offerings, a facility that provided a very real identity for LTI in the Lexington and greater central Kentucky community.

Modern amenities seemed to abound when the Oswald Building opened its spacious quarters. The building had three stories, was fire resistant thanks to a contemporary automatic sprinkler system, and was

▲ Lexington Technical Institute, Oswald Building, ca. 1976.

▲ The Oswald Building lobby.

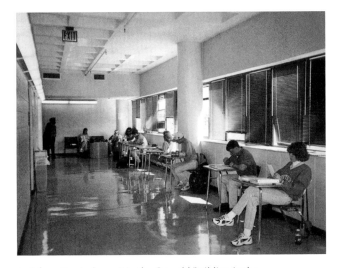

▲ A favorite study spot in the Oswald Building is the end of the third floor hallway toward Chevy Chase.

constructed in a "monolithic pattern" of structurally reinforced concrete columns, floors, and ceilings, as described in the 1980 *LTI Self-Study*. Exterior design featured concrete panels alternating with glass, an edifice clearly reflective of its place in time. Originally there was 31,198 square feet dedicated to classroom space, with faculty and administrative offices, shops, laboratories, vocational areas, and the school library taking up the most footage with 41,619 square feet. Oswald Building's address was placed at 500 Cooper Drive.

Truly one of the most important new additions to the Institute came with the Oswald Building's capacity to house a library geared specifically to LTI students and programs. For the first twelve years of operation, LTI had no library it could call its own. In the autumn of 1976, all that changed. According to the 1980 *LTI Self-Study*, many Institute faculty believed the new library was as important an achievement in attaining status and identity as was the Oswald Building itself that housed it. By

> *All those tied to LTI welcomed the opening in 1976 of the new John W. Oswald Building, ...the actual date that marked when LTI "really" got started as a distinct institution.*

the end of the 1970s, the LTI library could count some 170 periodicals at its disposal, and some 4,500 materials in its collections. One of the results of the *LTI Self-Study* of 1980 for reaccreditation by the Southern Association of Colleges and Schools was a call for substantial expansion of the library. The study recommended a considerable increase of serials from 170 to 300, and a very substantial expansion in general books and related materials from 4,500 to at least 32,000. While access to the University of Kentucky libraries alleviated much of this shortfall, and while the LTI library did hold materials to "provide broad coverage," the 1980 study pointed out a present "lack of depth of coverage" in overall holdings and insisted upon upgrades.

Enlarged programs and ever-increasing numbers of students required more and more LTI faculty and staff. By the late 1970s, the school employed dozens of full-time faculty members. One of those held an earned Ed.D., and one held a D.M.D. The 1980 self-study reported

▲ Before computer search engines streamed instant answers to inquiries, there was the trusty card catalog—trusty, but slow.

▲ Martha Birchfield, Cindy Leonard, Larry Chiswell, Pat Lefler, and Karen Clark in an "early" Oswald Building faculty pow-wow.

▲ Jim Connell teaches a session in electrical engineering.

twenty-nine faculty members held master's degrees, with another eight with earned bachelor's degrees as their top academic credential, two with associate degrees, and one faculty member held no academic degree.

Fayette County continued to be the home base for the LTI service area, although several unique programs offered by the Institute, such as architectural technology and the well-established dental laboratory technology program, drew students not only from other parts of central Kentucky but also from around the state, and even other parts of the country. As an added benefit, students at LTI, and indeed residents generally throughout the community, could avail themselves of career counseling services at the Institute. Developmental studies offered by LTI helped prepare many students with deficient preparation for college level work, particularly in the basic skills of reading, writing, and arithmetic. Far too many high school graduates in Kentucky, and elsewhere for that matter, for whatever reasons, did not receive the sort of preparation necessary to begin college studies. Developmental studies courses gave these students new hope and opportunities to pursue their dreams, even a wholly new outlook on life. Providing these avenues of preparation to students demonstrated the Institute's commitment to "fulfill its mission as a 'community' college, open to everyone who can benefit from services and programs offered by the college," stated the 1980 *LTI Self-Study*.

> By 1979, LTI had eighteen technical programs, organized under three separate divisions, with an enrollment total of 2,074 students.

Whether remedial, compensatory, or developmental in nature, the education of the "academically underprivileged" student was taken seriously at LTI, as were those identified by authors Milton Spann, Jr., and Suella McCrimmon, in editor George Baker's *A Handbook on the Community College in America* (1994) as "learning disabled, the visually and hearing impaired, the mobility handicapped, the English as a Second Language student, the student-athlete, the returning adult student, and the first generation student." Ultimately, all could find a safe haven in the community college setting.

Well before cultural diversity, multiculturalism, and pluralism became higher education standards to be measured and goals to be achieved, the student body of LTI reflected a wide range of backgrounds not previously seen on more traditional college campuses. LTI students hailed from many different experiences and circumstances, some full-time and some part-time, some single, some married, many nontraditional in the sense of being older than the 18-to-25 age range, some seeking degrees, some not, some taking courses in the evening rather than the day, some living on campus and some commuting. In fact, the LTI student body by the late 1970s showed more than half over age twenty-five, and the majority employed either full- or part-time, according to the 1980 *LTI Self-Study*. For the fall 1980 semester, there was a mix of 904 males to 1,207 females, 30 students from out of state, 21 foreign, 1,888 Caucasians, 176 African Americans, 10 American Indians, 8 Asian Americans, and 7 Hispanic Americans, according to the *Compendium of Selected Data & Characteristics 1980–81.* Statistics were not available for sexual orientation, but certainly there was at least the typical percentage of gay/lesbian/bisexual/transgender students in the college population that one might expect in the general population, usually set somewhere between 5 and 10 percent. All together, it was a rather impressive mix for the times, with even more impressive strides yet to come.

By 1979, LTI had eighteen technical programs, organized under three separate divisions, with an enrollment total of 2,074 students. All eighteen programs were geared toward attainment of an associate in applied science degree. Unsurprisingly, some programs flourished while others languished and ultimately faded away. The Forest and Wood Technology program, actually started as a UK Community College System program where the first year of general courses was offered at LTI, showed a decrease in enrollment figures for the second year of study, which required a year in residence at or near Quicksand, in Breathitt County. Waning numbers meant no new students were admitted to the program for the fall 1980 semester, and the program would be phased out once all those enrolled had completed their course of study. Similarly, the Fire Science Technology

Civil engineering surveying class.

▲ UK Housing accommodated hundreds of LTI and LCC students.

program, started in 1973 largely due to the urging of local fire departments to provide college training specifically to firefighters, also was experiencing declining enrollments and thus was reported in the 1980 *LTI Self-Study* as scheduled for closure in the 1980–81 academic year.

These programs reflected an LTI answer to specific community needs, particularly in terms of workforce preparation. Just as community needs changed over time, the Institute programs would likewise change to reflect a response to those needs. Helping decide what new programs might be offered at the Institute and what programs discontinued were various program advisory committees, made up of individuals with expertise and interest in the specific program in question. A common fixture in community colleges generally, the Program Advisory Committee role, as described in the 1980 self-study, included curriculum planning and design, devising program objectives, creating placement programs for students in cooperative education programs, recommending community service and continuing education projects, and providing for or assisting in job placement for graduates. These committees provided the broad leadership required for program design and development. From there, faculty took up the lead to prepare students for the rigors of the marketplace. By the early 1980s, few could question the success of the LTI faculty, indeed the whole enterprise, in its preparation of students for employment.

A community college can mean many different things to many different people. In the beginning, the institutional purpose of the Lexington Technical Institute was to focus, as the name implied, on technical programs, particularly in the health sciences, and award Associate in Applied Science degrees to graduates. Then in 1984 came the great change of LTI to a comprehensive community college. Under University of Kentucky president Dr. Otis Singletary, UK by the early 1980s was moving toward implementation of a selective admissions policy. Up to this point, any Kentucky high school graduate who applied could gain admission to the University of Kentucky undergraduate program. But in 1983, the UK Board of Trustees voted to end open admissions and begin a selective admissions process based upon academic criteria and performance. This meant that many aspiring UK students, many the sons and daughters of UK alumni, would not be admitted to the University because of academic or other shortfalls.

One means of circumnavigating these obstructive waters, or otherwise skirting the new policy, depending on one's point of view, was to expand the LTI mission to take on the status of a comprehensive community college. Open admissions would continue at all Kentucky community colleges statewide. Up to now, LTI had not needed to offer general education courses, such as political science, history, sociology, or chemistry, since LTI students had access to those courses through the University. That was about to change. In 1984, selective admissions went into effect at UK. That same year, the University of Kentucky Lexington Technical Institute became the University of Kentucky Lexington Community College, a comprehensive community college charged to serve the greater Lexington and central Kentucky community, just as its sister institutions did in other settings across the state.

Big changes were about to begin for the Institute newly styled as a College. Lexington Community College took on a three-fold mission: (1) awarding associate degrees in career-oriented technical programs, (2) providing transferable pre-baccalaureate course work, and (3) providing continuing education and community service activities as needed, as outlined in the 2000 *LCC Self-Study*. Institutional purpose was spelled out in more detail in the 1990 *LCC Self-Study* for the Southern Association of Colleges and Schools. Specifically, the mission was defined as follows:

▲ Janet Sanford, Radiography, '74, LCC. Radiation Therapy Tech., UK Medical Center, Lexington, Kentucky.

▲ Judy McLaughlin teaches radiological technology.

The Lexington Community College is a comprehensive college which has a threefold comprehensive mission; that is

1. To offer career-oriented programs designed to prepare students for immediate technical or semi-professional employment. These programs are usually completed in two years and are composed of about one-half general education courses and the other half semi-professional or technical education classes. The Associate in Applied Science Degree is awarded upon completion of the curriculum.

2. To offer curricula for the first two years of a baccalaureate program. Courses parallel University offerings and are transferable to the Lexington campus of the University of Kentucky or to another four-year institution either public or private. At the conclusion of the prescribed curriculum, the Associate in Arts Degree or Associate in Science Degree may be awarded.

3. To provide general educational opportunities for citizens in their immediate areas. These

programs include evening classes, workshops, seminars, short courses, concert series, exhibits, lectures, dramatic presentations and festivals to meet in-service, re-education and cultural needs of the community.
(1990 LCC Self-Study)

◄ Early LCC logo.

Defining its mission gave greater strength to the institution, and provided clarity of purpose to all those associated with Lexington Community College, or LCC as it became popularly known, on whatever level. Certainly one thing such statements are meant to accomplish includes an explanation to students about just where it is they are going with their studies. What was missing was an understanding that the students were being prepared for more than just rote practice of learned skills or behaviors in their jobs. Instead, "the college strives to ensure that all students are 'intellectually flexible, articulate, creative, and prepared for continuous growth,'" as stated in the *Lexington Community College Catalog 1999–2000*. Still, the objective to transform the student into a lifelong learner sometimes gets lost. Oftentimes it takes years, if it happens, for that epiphany to occur that tells one that one's education actually made sense.

UNIVERSITY OF KENTUCKY
COMMUNITY COLLEGE SYSTEM
BRECKINRIDGE HALL
LEXINGTON. KENTUCKY 40506-0056

OFFICE OF THE VICE PRESIDENT

October 8, 1982

Dr. Otis A. Singletary, President
103 Administration Building
CAMPUS 00323

Dear President Singletary:

Per your instructions, I have worked with Art Gallaher on the changes necessary for L.T.I. to move to comprehensive community college status. Unless you have objection, I will proceed in the direction outlined below. My plan essentially calls for L.T.I. to assume the responsibility for the general education of its present students beginning summer 1983 and to enroll transfer students beginning summer 1984. Should the Lexington Campus move to selective admissions for 1983-84, my proposed schedule would have to be altered to enroll transfer students in summer 1983.

In the <u>administrative</u> area, L.T.I. will handle the entire admission and registration process beginning summer 1983. Fees will be assessed and collected in 1983 by the same process presently followed by the other 12 colleges. As a part of the reorganization effort, L.T.I. will have the responsibility for its maintenance and operations beginning sometime during the present fall semester. Campus safety and security and "outside the building" maintenance, groundskeeping, etc., will continue to be provided by the Lexington Campus, per the reorganization agreement. In short, with the change, L.T.I. will provide essentially the same programs and services currently in place at the other 12 colleges.

In the <u>student services</u> area, L.T.I. students will continue to pay the same activity fee paid by all Lexington Campus students. The funds collected from this fee, part of the tuition for L.T.I. students, will be transmitted annually from Community College System income to an appropriate income account in the University System. By paying the activity fee, all L.T.I. students will have a U.K. I.D. card and continue to be eligible for the full range of student services available to all other U.K. students in Lexington, including dining. Students enrolled in occupational programs will be eligible for U.K. housing; students in the transfer program will not.

In the <u>curriculum</u> area, the general education courses needed for L.T.I. students will be planned and offered by L.T.I. beginning with summer 1983. During 1982-83, existing space in L.T.I. originally planned for "wet" laboratories will be converted to Chemistry, Biology, and Physics Labs. L.T.I. will then be able to offer the science courses needed for 1983-84.

Dr. Otis A. Singletary, President
Page Two
October 8, 1982

Art and I have agreed that it would be appropriate for L.T.I. to consider employing some graduate students from the Lexington Campus to assist with part-time instruction in general education, particularly in the sciences. With its present enrollment, L.T.I. is already very tightly scheduled for classroom and faculty office space. I will identify any space needs and work with Art Gallaher to identify space, if available, on the Lexington Campus to house general classroom and office needs until L.T.I. facilities can be expanded. Chancellor Gallaher and I have agreed that there will be no automatic cross registration or enrollment between L.T.I. and the Lexington Campus. We do plan to honor existing agreements whereby L.T.I. offers certain courses for Lexington Campus students and, of course, plan to allow students to apply and be accepted to take courses in both the Lexington Campus and L.T.I. if admission requirements can be met on both campuses.

I propose to implement this change with the tuition income generated by L.T.I. students, less the activity fee portion, that is presently included in the Lexington Campus budget. While I realize that this amount is not sufficient to fund a general education program at L.T.I., Chancellor Gallaher can make a good case for the fact that general education instruction for L.T.I. students is presently being provided by part-time faculty and graduate students out of the tuition income. Art and I will work with the Central Administration Budget Office to identify the tuition income in question. Once agreement is reached on the amount, that income will be budgeted in the Community College System beginning July 1, 1983.

The steps outlined above for academic year 1983-84 can be implemented without Board action and without the necessity for approval from outside the University. Assuming selective admissions for the Lexington Campus in fall 1984, I will propose, at the appropriate time agreed to by you, that U.K. Board approval be sought to change L.T.I. to comprehensive community college status, reporting to the Chancellor for the Community College System, to enable transfer students to be enrolled there in summer 1984. In my opinion, that change, under existing statute, can be made by the U.K. Board without "outside the University" approval.

Sincerely,

Charles T. Wethington, Jr.

rlc

Enclosures

cc: Art Gallaher
    Don Clapp

Planning for the transition from Lexington Technical Institute to Lexington Community College started early. Here is a letter from Charles T. Wethington, Jr., vice president of the University of Kentucky Community College System, to University of Kentucky President Otis Singletary on the plan to reorganize LTI.

Along with a new name and an expanded mission, the University of Kentucky Lexington Community College saw some administrative changes take place. In 1984, LTI Director Bill Price moved on, replaced by only the second woman to head a Kentucky community college up to that time, Associate Director Sharon B. Jaggard. Jaggard was an Indiana native with bachelor of science and master of science degrees from Indiana State University, and a Ph.D. from Pennsylvania State University. Before her selection in 1983 as associate director of LTI, Jaggard had served in the UK Community College System Professional Development office. When the transition took place in 1984 creating Lexington Community College, Jaggard was chosen as the first director of the new College. "Shay," as she was called, apparently had not been the first choice for director among the LCC faculty, but she was chosen nevertheless, which inevitably led to some unfortunate tension between her and most of the faculty.

Jaggard told the *Lexington Herald-Leader* on June 28, 1984, that Lexington Community College would "have a new kind of student clientele and some new faculty... in the humanities and the liberal arts, which we haven't had." Jaggard faced the potentially daunting task of making the LTI-LCC transition work smoothly. She led several discussions with faculty and staff along these very lines, such as those during the October 22–23, 1984, Administrative Staff retreat at Carnahan House, where Jaggard noted in her October 26 newsletter, *Director's Brief*, that the College situation was to be carefully examined, including "our assumptions about the various components of the college and about our public, and an identification of the major issues facing us. . . ."

In the November 5, 1984, issue of the newsletter, Jaggard thought it "exciting" that so many faculty and staff employed microcomputers as instructional tools, quite an innovation for that time. (For perspective, the first IBM personal computer, or IBM PC, rolled off the assembly line in 1981.) Jaggard expressed her desire to modernize the administrative offices with computer technology. She noted that she had received many requests from faculty and staff for additional microcomputers, and that she had "activated" a College Computer Advisory Committee "to be a review and advisory 'sounding' board on future microcomputer purchases."

Business and security issues also were addressed in the director's newsletter that November. Jaggard made clear her full support of the new Assistant Director of Business Affairs, Marilyn Childre, and

▲ Della White, Jim Embry, Marilyn Childre, and Dorothy Hall take a moment to pose.

the latter's assignment to certain "critical" issues of building operation and maintenance, processing of documents, and other issues. "You probably need to know that I did direct last week that the building be locked on football weekends," wrote Jaggard. "We have experienced vandalism and the risk of personal liabilities. Non-football weekends will be available to you as usual," she promised.

But other challenges beleaguered the director. In the November 16, 1984, newsletter, Jaggard thought it necessary to reassure all faculty and staff: "No, the college is not bankrupt. No, the college is not being closed. These and similar amusing rumors can be put to rest." Advanced registration was cancelled, however, because it "had become an administrative nightmare which no longer served the purpose for which it was designed.... Let me not bore you with the details," Jaggard wrote, while making it clear that the "prepayment process" caused an "accounts receivable" problem that was apparently "unmanageable."

Other newsletter reports were more positive. A new LCC Advisory Board met August 19, 1985, including Dr. John Smith, Mr. Jack Boehm, Sister Michael Leo Mullaney, Mr. Larry Martini, Mr. Richard Blanchard, Mr. Lewis Owens, Ms. Martha Birchfield, Mr. Tim Garnett, Dr. Charles Wethington, and Jaggard. That same date, the Fayette County Public Schools Board opened rooms at Bryan Station High School in Lexington's north end to LCC for class offerings. A three-foot, ten-inch-tall, "several hundred pounds" weight computer, an IBM System/36, was delivered to the College and scheduled for installation on August 23. A new Word Processing Center was opened. Not everyone had been pleased with the idea of creating the center, but most seemed to accept it and even like it soon after opening. Debbie Holt, Gloria Eckler, Margaret Greatbatch, and Nona Sparks were singled out as responsible for the new center's set-up and success. The following semester welcomed another technological improvement with the college's "first online computerized registration."

> **A three-foot, ten-inch-tall, "several hundred pounds" weight computer, an IBM System/36, was delivered to the College and scheduled for installation on August 23 [1985]. A new Word Processing Center was opened.**

But Jaggard's two-year stay as director did not bring about improved relations between herself and the faculty. It seemed there was a failure to communicate. "As everyone must know by now, one of the major priorities for the college this year is to improve communications... An outside consultant will lead the assessment and analysis of our communications and will be on campus," specifically Dr. James Hammons, a professor of higher education at the University of Arkansas. Jaggard hoped that Hammons, with his extensive community college experience and fine academic and administrative credentials, might help improve her situation at LCC. But it did not work. Often it seemed she was busily engaged in "putting out fires," a notion made clear even through the newsletter. Whatever the reason or reasons, Jaggard announced her resignation rather abruptly during a meeting in 1986 to take up a new job in Indianapolis.

Conceivably one of the most important things this change pointed up was that a director did not necessarily have great influence on the progress of the institution, at least in the estimation of one faculty member of the time, Larry Chiswell. Certainly the institution was larger than the person charged to steer it along its path. Considerable planning obviously took place prior to changing LTI to LCC, according to Marie Piekarski. With the addition of general education courses and the comprehensive community college mission, LCC growth accelerated. Perhaps the College machine, the quality of the faculty and staff, the efficacy of instruction, was more important to the school's success than a director or a president or a name.

Stepping in as interim director was Dr. Ben Carr, Jr. A native of Harlan, Kentucky, Carr started his UK career in 1972 when he joined the LTI faculty as an engineering technology instructor. Before he moved on to the Community College System Office, Carr served as associate director of LTI. For his professional training, Carr earned bachelor's and master's degrees in electrical engineering before receiving his doctorate in higher education, all degrees coming from UK. For about half of 1986, Carr was LCC interim director. In the *Director's Briefcase* newsletter (the newsletter had been renamed the year before), Carr acknowledged his appreciation for the "warm welcome" from faculty and staff. "I need your help," wrote Carr, "in making this transition a smooth and orderly process with no interruption in the good teaching-learning climate which exists here."

Carr reported that the Visiting Committee for the College's Five-Year Unit Review, which conducted an examination of the College in January 1985 for the purpose of institutional self-study and analysis of

▼ Allen G. Edwards, Ph.D., last LCC director and first president of Lexington Community College. 2001UA028:1330, University of Kentucky Archives

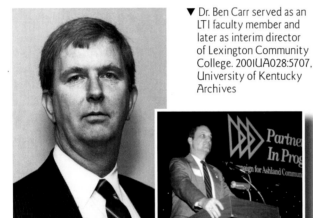

▼ Dr. Ben Carr served as an LTI faculty member and later as interim director of Lexington Community College. 2001UA028:5707, University of Kentucky Archives

operations in preparation for the 1990 SACS self-study and reaffirmation of accreditation, had completed their report. The Visiting Committee "found LCC to be a viable and dynamic institution. The Committee members had many good things to say" about LCC, Carr noted, "especially the strong faculty and staff." Carr lauded the benefits of such a study, and congratulated all those who "contributed your energy and time to the Unit Review process. . . Once again, the College has joined together to accomplish a difficult task."

Carr did not remain long in his role of acting director. Once relieved of his interim duties, he returned to his post as vice chancellor of the UK Community College System, where he served under Chancellor Charles Wethington. Taking up his mantle was the associate director of LCC, Dr. Allen G. Edwards. Edwards came from Gibson, North Carolina, and graduated with a B.A. in 1971 from Clemson University. After graduation, he worked as a recruiter and instructor at Chesterfield and Marlboro Technical College in South Carolina. In 1973, he moved to Midlands Technical College in Columbia, South Carolina, where he taught English and developmental studies. In 1975, Edwards received a master's degree in education from the University of South Carolina, and in 1984, he completed his Ph.D. at the University of Texas at Austin.

Edwards came to Lexington in June 1985 as associate director for academic affairs at Lexington Community College. In 1986, upon becoming director, Edwards expressed his pleasure in the *Director's*

▲ Left to right, Bonnie Pagen, Gail Carpenter, Anne Noffsinger, Judy Rutledge, Peyton Gooch, and Irene Hume.

▲ Architectural Technology class ACH 100–Introduction to Drafting and Blueprint Reading, fall 1987, in the Oswald Building.

Briefcase: "I can't tell you how delighted I am to be the new Director of Lexington Community College. I am grateful for the opportunity to work with the faculty and staff of this college in my new role. I appreciate your support during this past year; I will need it more than ever in the years to come." Edwards enjoyed a stronger entrance than his predecessor. A new building was in the works; a "Community Development Component" was underway; and the reputation of the College was improving and spreading. Edwards hoped to "maintain" that "reputation for good teaching and strong technical and transfer programs."

Edwards seemed to hit the ground running. For example, he announced the formation of a "Committee 2000" made up of faculty, staff, and advisory board members who were charged to serve as "a steering committee for the College." Made up of Bob Blake, Dick Blanchard, Helene Chlopan, Larry Chiswell, Arvin Jupin, Pat Lefler, Dennis Marshall, Anne Noffsinger, Lewis Owens, Joe Phillips, Scott Secrist, Larry Stanley, Patsy Stice, Barbara White, and the yet unnamed associate director and business/industry liaison, they were "asked to help

A new building was in the works... the reputation of the College was improving and spreading.

us focus on long-range goals and priorities" for the College. Specifically, they were to address three areas:

1. To identify key community members who, through a series of forums, panels, [and] colloquia, can advise [LCC] on emerging technologies and trends in health, business, engineering, and the humanities.

2. To examine the emerging technologies and trends to determine how [LCC] should prepare in terms of time, space, resources, organization, procedures, and outcomes.

3. To advise [the LCC director] on priorities for the College in getting and allocating resources for the future.

A September 1986 *Chronicle of Higher Education* story on "Change in America" emphasized the need for such planning. Specifically, the article focused on the change underway in work and the workforce, where it would lead by 2000, and what higher education must do to meet the challenge. Forecasts predicted an older workforce, a smaller percentage number of those aged sixteen to twenty-four years, a growing minority workforce, and a huge challenge to retrain many workers. "By the year 2000," the *Chronicle* reported, "75 percent of all workers currently employed will need retraining." These and other projections made the Committee 2000 studies all the more important.

Some programs, already well established, seemed to continue to shine. For example, the Dental Laboratory Technology students could rightly be proud of scoring the second highest grades in the nation on the "National Board for Certification in Dental Laboratory Technology 1986 Recognized Graduate Examination." The newsletter congratulated Dental Lab faculty members Art Dameron, Morris Fields, Robin Gornto, and Don Shear for their fine teaching and preparation of students.

Nursing, the other original LTI mainstay program of the College, hosted a National League for Nursing (NLN) team on a site visit the previous October. The November newsletter told of an exit interview that was "a positive, informative exchange." Commendations from the team came on several fronts: good clinical sites, "qualified and caring" faculty, a "positive environment" for students, and the "leadership" provided by Dr. Anne Noffsinger.

In August 1986, LCC began to advertise itself in earnest as a community college for the first time, taking out advertising space in *Lexington Herald-Leader* supplements, and broadcasting local radio spots featuring the popular voice of the Kentucky Wildcats, Cawood Ledford, a sure hook for the many Kentucky Wildcat fans inhabiting the Bluegrass. Classes would be offered for the first time in four of the counties surrounding Fayette for the fall 1986 semester, including Bourbon, Clark, Jessamine, and Woodford. All these additional course offerings placed additional strains on the Registrar's office, an office then in transition. To continue the solid administrative base provided by able and meticulous Registrar Richard Greissman, the equally capable and detail-oriented Pat Lefler stepped up to the call. Later, Becky Harp-Stephens would carry on the tradition of solid administration from the Registrar's perch.

Edwards gave his readers of the January 1987 College newsletter an intimate glimpse of his thinking as an educator when he addressed them with the theme of renewal:

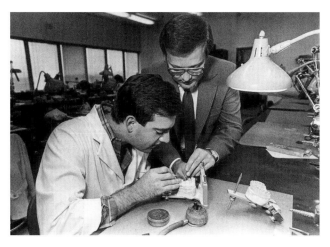

▲ Professor Art Dameron instructs a student on the finer points in dental laboratory technology.

I always begin the new year with mixed emotions—sadness about being older and missed opportunities; happiness from being given another chance. At least I hope that I have learned to give up the fear of the future and to forge ahead in 1987. As someone said, life is the art of drawing without an eraser. After the 1960 World Series, Yogi Berra answered a reporter's question about defeat by saying, "We made too many wrong mistakes." I hope that I don't make too many wrong mistakes this year....

Renewal, like learning, tends to occur more readily in those who have a positive attitude toward the future. It occurs most readily in those who are not afraid of change. People need change. In the Greek myth, Sisyphus was condemned to spend eternity in Hades pushing a stone up a hill. When he reached the top, the stone broke loose and rolled down and he had to start over again. The problem was not that he had to keep pushing stones up hills. What made it Hell was that it was always the same stone, always the same hill. With different stones, different hills, it would have been bearable. Fortunately, we can choose different stones or, at least, different hills each year. The nature of education is that it invites change in both student and teacher. I hope that 1987 will be a year of growth and renewal for us all.

One way, perhaps, that faculty could take up the call for change in 1987 was to apply for a Summer Teaching Improvement Fellowship offered to full-time faculty members by the Community College System Office. Up to $2,000 was available in an award, designated to assist projects in course improvement, program design, evaluation of "intervention strategies," redesign of an existing course, and development of instructional resources, as stated by the January newsletter. Another avenue for improvement made possible in 1987 came when LCC began to offer weekend classes for the first time. Faculty member Carolyn Beam developed new programs in medical transcription, and she explored other possible offerings working with community organizations. From the private sector, thanks went out to IBM for being "very generous in providing expertise and guidance in planning for the future of our college." Another expression of gratitude was merited by a private gift, given in March 1987, by LTI/LCC graduate Scott Secrist, who "offered to donate about $100,000 worth of equipment to the Nuclear Medicine Program," the same program he graduated from and taught in for several years.

Procedural change came through the College administration when they introduced a management philosophy and mathematical tracking method long

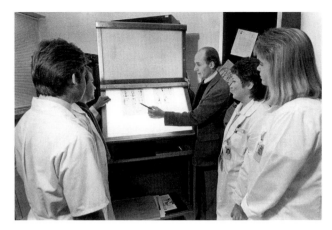

▲ Scott Secrist teaches class.

used by the manufacturing sector in industry, called statistical process control, or SPC. The College newsletter in January 1987 noted that "the entire purpose of entering into this process is to improve the quality of service we provide to the public." Dr. Edwards believed the introduction of SPC techniques to the faculty and staff to be perhaps "the single most important event to occur on this campus this year." SPC certainly reflected the administrative penchant to collect information and quantify College personnel activities.

▲ Registrar Richard Greissman presides during a staff meeting.

LCC in literary form.

LEXINGTON HERALD-LEADER

Community

News of Fayette, Bourbon, Clark, Franklin, Jessamine, Madison, Scott and Woodford counties

Lexington, Ky.

June 12, 199

MAKING the GRADE

Mother takes top honors at LCC, fulfills dream with support from family

By Suzanne Froelich
Contributing writer

When Marty Surbaugh, a 40-year-old mother of three, enrolled in Lexington Community College three years ago, questions clouded her dream of becoming a dental hygienist.

Was she too old to keep up with the 18-year-olds? Would her household fall apart if she wasn't there to cook, clean and organize? What would her friends say if she failed?

Surbaugh not only made it but also received an academic scholarship after her first semester. At graduation May 3, she was named the top student in a class of 340.

In addition, she was named to a 20-member Academic All-American Second Team. She was selected from more than 400 nominees nationwide by Phi Theta Kappa fraternity in cooperation with the American Association of Community and Junior Colleges and USA Today.

Surbaugh's 3.89 grade point average (on a 4.0 scale) contributed to these distinctions, but other qualities were judged as well, said Paul Taylor, dean of students at LCC.

"Marty studies hard and applies herself, but she is also enthusiastic and committed to the college and the students here," he said. "She is always ready to help. Marty is a real role model."

Surbaugh served on a student-faculty appeals board that resolved student complaints at LCC. "I was the same age as some of the faculty, but I had a student's perspective," she said.

And for the last two summers, she has advised incoming students as part of a college survival course offered by LCC.

> **Making a difference in Fayette County**

Dental hygienist Marty Surbaugh at her office in Lexington: "The first time I worked with a patient, I knew I had done the right thing," she said.

Herald-Leader/Tim Sharp

Please see GRADE, 8

Dental Hygiene student gains recognition for her achievements, *Lexington Herald-Leader*, June 12, 1991.

▲ Dr. Edwards, left, presents a public speaking award to Kathy Aldridge while Carl Leonard of McGraw-Hill publishing company assists and communications professor Peggy Allen looks on.

Sometimes it seemed important to highlight a national study or trend to the faculty, perhaps to lend greater perspective to the consequence of classroom instruction, such as the article written by the American Council on Education senior fellow Dr. Harold L. Hodgkinson, published in the December 1986 issue of the *Phi Delta Kappan*, entitled "Reform? Higher Education? Don't be Absurd!" Hodgkinson characterized the state of American higher education as in "scandalous condition," with plummeting scores on the SAT, one of the two premier standardized admissions tests for college, and the GRE, or Graduate Record Examination, taken by college graduates for admission to graduate school. Hodgkinson also pointed out that "Almost all the student diversity in higher education—by ethnicity, age, and cultural background—is handled by community colleges. These institutions," he continued, "seldom receive any rewards for this difficult task. Indeed, they are often thought of as 'second rate' because they have taken the issue of student diversity seriously and acted accordingly." Many LCC faculty members could confirm these misguided opinions from experience.

Guest speakers often provided a fresh perspective to issues facing the College, the community, and the country at large. Faculty, staff, and students were urged in the January newsletter to attend an April 21, 1987, event in the Oswald auditorium, room 230, featuring Dr. Peter P. Bosomworth, Chancellor of the UK Medical Center, and Sister Michael Leo Mullaney, of the Roman Catholic Sisters of Charity of Nazareth order and for twenty-one years head of Lexington's oldest and largest private hospital, St. Joseph's. Speakers in the Committee 2000 Health Forum, they were going to begin with an outline of the dramatic changes that had taken place over the last five years in the health care industry, driven especially by changes in insurance laws and technology. Their vision of medical care in the year 2000 followed, aimed at "how well we, as educators, identify and adapt to change," and addressed specifically the importance of "well prepared nurses, therapists, and technicians" in that future environment. Such topics resonated well with LCC audiences.

Edwards, who took up the title of LCC president in 1988, the first of the College's administrators to hold that designation, faced many of the same problems as his predecessors, but most especially he, along with the faculty and staff, had to deal with the College's booming enrollment. Enrollment had doubled since the mid-1980s, from 2,538 in 1985 to 4,985 in 1991, according to the *Compendium of Selected Data & Characteristics 1991–92*.

TABLE 9
Average Salaries by Rank for Teaching Faculty
Lexington Community College

Year	Professor	Associate Professor	Assistant Professor	Instructor	All Ranks
1980-81	20,894 (2)	20,513 (6)	15,424 (28)	13,949 (17)	15,733 (53)
1981-82	23,594 (2)	21,742 (8)	17,131 (33)	14,623 (14)	17,389 (57)
1982-83	24,339 (3)	22,509 (12)	17,413 (32)	15,938 (13)	18,459 (60)
1983-84	26,487 (2)	22,961 (18)	17,624 (28)	17,108 (21)	19,116 (69)
1984-85	27,481 (3)	22,438 (21)	17,516 (36)	16,340 (12)	19,171 (72)
1985-86	29,714 (3)	24,022 (27)	19,742 (33)	18,688 (11)	21,551 (74)
1986-87	31,725 (5)	25,454 (32)	21,172 (27)	18,875 (14)	23,193 (78)
1987-88	35,031 (6)	26,020 (33)	22,117 (20)	22,053 (13)	24,970 (72)
1988-89	35,447 (5)	26,651 (32)	22,362 (21)	21,158 (17)	24,791 (75)

Sources: University of Kentucky Community College System. *Compendia of Selected Data and Characteristics*, 1981-1989.

▲ 1990 Self-Study: Average Salaries by Rank for Teaching Faculty.

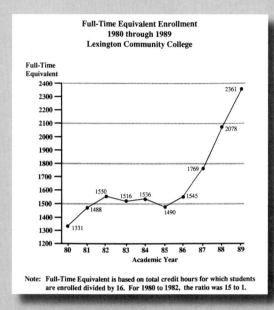

**Full-Time Equivalent Enrollment
1980 through 1989
Lexington Community College**

Note: Full-Time Equivalent is based on total credit hours for which students are enrolled divided by 16. For 1980 to 1982, the ratio was 15 to 1.

▲ 1990 Self-Study: Full-Time Equivalent Enrollment, 1980 through 1989.

**TABLE 5
Number of Graduates by Technical Programs
Lexington Community College**

	1979-1980	1980-1981	1981-1982	1982-1983	1983-1984	1984-1985	1985-1986	1986-1987	1987-1988	1988-1989
Accounting Tech.	14	22	19	17	16	17	26	21	19	8
Architectural Tech.	25	21	24	30	24	17	18	26	29	19
Business Tech.	18	34	30	22	45	51	46	36	39	28
Civil Engineering Tech.	2	7	8	1	2	7	5	4		
Data Processing Tech.	12	17	28	48	70	59	43	31	23	19
Dental Hygiene	15	15	12	14	8	9	15	9	13	14
Dental Lab Tech.	21	14	11	18	18	15	17	14	16	12
Engineering Tech.										
Electrical	19	12	23	20	27	21	29	25	23	18
Mechanical	4	6	7	4	8	7	9	3	6	6
Fire Science Tech.	3	1	1							
Forest and Wood Tech.			1		1					
Nuclear Medicine Tech.	4			8		6	3	4	4	4
Nursing	68	57	86	79	77	83	56	69	46	57
Office Administration	25	26	33	28	50	40	38	29	33	26
Radiologic Tech.	20	15	14	11	14	15	12	19	16	11
Real Estate	6*		4	6	6	6	4	5	14	8
Respiratory Care	16	16	16	14	17	15	16	13	7	9
Transportation Tech.	5	2	3	1**	1**					
Other	1	1			8					
TOTAL	278	266	320	321	392	368	337	308	288	239

*Management Technology, Real Estate Option
**Management Technology, Transportation Option

Sources: University of Kentucky Community College System and Lexington Community College Office of Institutional Research. *Compendia of Selected Data and Characteristics*, 1981-1989.

**TABLE 6
Associate Degree Requirements
Number of Credit Hours Required
Lexington Community College**

	Writing	Oral Comm	Math	Bio/Phys Science	History/ Human	Soc/Beh Science	Major Req	Elective	Total
Accounting Technology	9	3	6	3	3	6	30	6	66
Architectural Technology	6	3	3	3	3	3	48	1-3	70-72
Business Technology									
Management	6	3	6	3	3	6	37-39	1-3	65-69
Retail Marketing	6	3	6	3	3	6	37-39	1-3	65-69
Computer Info. Systems									
Microcomputer	6	3	3-6	3	3	3	39-42	3	66
Programming	6	3	3	3	3	3	42	3	66
Dental Hygiene	6	3	3	15	3	6	37	1-3	74-76
Dental Lab Technology	6	3	3	6-9	3	3	44	1-3	69-74
Engineering Technology									
Electrical	6	3	9	10	3	3	36	1-3	71-73
Mechanical	6	3	9	8	3	3	38	1-3	71-73
Nuclear Med. Technology	6	3	3	17-18	3	3-4	33	1-3	69-73
Nursing	6	3	3	12-13	3	9-10	32	1-3	69-73
Office Administration	6	3	3	3	3	6-7	41	1-3	66-69
Radiologic Technology	6	3	3	11	3	6-7	35	1-3	68-71
Real Estate	6	3	3	3	3	6	36-39	1-3	61-66
Respiratory Care	6	3	3	11-12	3	3-4	36	3	68-70
Associate in Arts	3-6	3	3	6	12	6		24-27	60
Associate in Science	3-6	3	4	12	6	3		26-29	60

Sources: University of Kentucky Community College System *Catalog*, 1989-1990 and University of Kentucky Community College Council Minutes, 24 May 1989 and 21 Feb. 1990.

▲ 1990 Self-Study: Associate Degree Requirements.

▲ 1990 Self-Study: Number of Graduates by Technical Program.

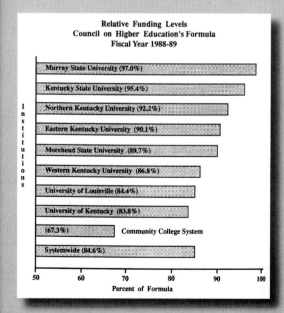

**Relative Funding Levels
Council on Higher Education's Formula
Fiscal Year 1988-89**

Murray State University (97.0%)
Kentucky State University (95.4%)
Northern Kentucky University (92.2%)
Eastern Kentucky University (90.1%)
Morehead State University (89.7%)
Western Kentucky University (86.8%)
University of Louisville (84.4%)
University of Kentucky (83.8%)
(67.3%) Community College System
Systemwide (84.6%)

Institutions

Percent of Formula

▲ 1990 Self-Study: Relative Funding Levels.

Despite real shortfalls in space, real progress for LCC could be registered in growth of the physical plant. In 1988, the Richard P. Moloney, Sr., Building, named for a late and important former Lexington area state legislator, opened on Cooper Drive. Thirty-eight thousand much-needed square feet were added to the College, including five computer laboratories, classrooms, a computer-aided drafting lab for architectural technology students, a darkroom, faculty offices, and a teleconference classroom on the first floor. University of Kentucky President David P. Roselle said during the dedication, attended by some 150 people, "This is a red-letter day for the University of Kentucky.... This building will make it possible for LCC to continue access to higher education." Kentucky State Senator Michael Moloney, son of the building's namesake, said his father would have been very proud.

Some additional space was found in the fall of 1990 to the tune of twenty thousand square feet in a building on Winchester Road in Lexington. According to the *Lexington Herald-Leader*, July 8, 1992, edition, however, it was definitely not a permanent solution. In a letter to the editor of the July 22, 1992, *Lexington Herald-Leader*, Edwards wrote that "overcrowded classrooms and unavailability of classes will be at an all-time high this coming semester because LCC lacks the resources to meet the demand for its services. We may turn away as many as 500 students this fall because we will not have enough faculty and

Artist's conception of the Moloney Building.

▼ Breaking ground for the Moloney Building, June 1987.

◀ University of Kentucky President David Roselle dedicated the Moloney Building in 1988.

staff.... I hope our overcrowding and lack of resources will be remedied soon." Edwards continued, "To do so will take the continued interest and efforts of the community, our legislative delegation, the University of Kentucky and the *Herald-Leader*. You can certainly count on me to do my part," closed Edwards.

Another building, the Academic Technical (AT) Building, joined the Oswald and Moloney structures in 1993 on the LCC mini-campus within the University. Ground was broken in January 1992 for the $3.4 million structure, to offer approximately forty thousand square feet of new space, including eighteen classrooms, forty faculty offices, a faculty lounge, and a student lounge, according to the *Herald-Leader*.

And there was a desire among many to make Lexington Community College the first choice for college freshmen and sophomores as well as those interested in the technical programs offered by the school. Some saw the College that way already. Twenty-three-year-old single mother of two Stephanie Wireman, a nursing student, said, "I think most people straight out of high school should go to a community college," reported the *Herald-Leader*, and her choice was LCC. Another student, twenty-five-year-old Lexington Henry Clay High School graduate David Carroll, wanted to go to UK but could not because of the University's selective admissions policy. "But since I've been in the community college system," he told reporters, "I would suggest it to any freshman coming in... You

Artist's conception of the Academic Technical Building.

have more one-on-one encounters with professors and teachers," another positive aspect of LCC's educational environment.

Of course, other resources were needed, too. "Simply put," reported the College newsletter, "we need more money, people, and equipment." In fact, all three of these areas would present a growing need in the College over the next several years. It would not be forty-eight-year-old Allen Edwards's problem: he announced in June 1993 that he had resigned to take the president's post at Pellissippi State Technical Community College in Knoxville, Tennessee. The College's long-range plan was devised, the new Academic Technical Building was to be dedicated in

July, and the College continued to expand. The LCC strategic plan called for increased efforts to become more independent in both name and function. Edwards told the *Lexington Herald-Leader* he wanted LCC to be identified by central Kentucky residents just like residents in Ashland, Hazard, and Paducah identified with their community colleges. But to achieve that end would be someone else's responsibility.

▼ Dr. Edwards at the dedication of the Academic Technical Building, 1993, while Ben Carr and Charles T. Wethington, Jr., look on.

◀ Dr. Edwards with Lewis Owen, editor of the *Lexington Herald-Leader*.

Still Bigger, Still Better

More than ever, Lexington area residents by the early 1990s recognized the acronym LCC to represent Lexington Community College. The College seemed to have great momentum on its side, with numbers and facilities larger and better than ever before, although space was barely adequate. The LCC connection with the University of Kentucky only enhanced the College's status within the central Kentucky community and gave it added prominence nationally as one of only a few such colleges tied to a major university. With its sister community colleges around Kentucky, the University of Kentucky Community College System achieved what many state "flagship" universities could only dream of, to wit: "'a statewide presence'. . . that no single campus could provide. . . ," as educational historian John R. Thelin observed in his work, *A History of American Higher Education* (2004). This geographical limitation was impossible to overcome in states like Indiana and California, noted Thelin. But in Kentucky, the community colleges' direct tie with the University of Kentucky gave UK an enormous presence and unparalleled influence statewide.

Unsurprisingly, in Lexington, the University of Kentucky dominates the landscape, and UK holds great, albeit not unlimited, sway in community affairs and in influence over community mood and outlook. But UK was not alone in importance. Students at UK and LCC could identify other institutions and landmarks that held tremendous influence in the community, such as the legendary Keeneland Race Course. Since 1936, Keeneland has held live horse race meets every April and October. A bastion of horseracing tradition, Keeneland in the spring meet hosts several races preparatory for the

◀ Two students enjoy a sunny day on the LCC campus lawn behind the Oswald Building.

◀ Charles T. Wethington, Jr., as tenth president of the University of Kentucky. 2001UA028:4974, University of Kentucky Archives

▲ Anthony Newberry (left) talks with former Kentucky Governor Edward T. "Ned" Breathitt.

famed Kentucky Derby, "The Run for the Roses," held in Louisville on the first Saturday in May since 1875, "The Most Exciting Two Minutes in Sports." Most of the scenes for the 2003 cinematic production *Seabiscuit*, set in 1938 and featuring the "Race of the Century" victory of Seabiscuit over highly favored 1937 Kentucky Derby winner War Admiral, were shot at Keeneland's stately racetrack. Kentuckians love a good horse race; in fact, they, like many others, enjoy races and athletic competition of various and sundry types.

An entirely different sort of competition faced LCC in 1993–94, when another search for a president got underway. Another year, another transition, or perhaps it so seemed. Since becoming a comprehensive community college in 1984, the school had witnessed what might be characterized as a revolving door at the top. UK Community College Chancellor Ben Carr, after promises to consult the LCC faculty for their input, announced appointment of a search committee for the president's post. According to the June 29, 1993, *Lexington Herald-Leader*, the committee would pare down the pack of applicants to ten or twelve contestants and then cull that down further to three finalists to recommend to the chancellor. Carr

would then send on one name to Charles Wethington, who had been appointed the tenth president of the University of Kentucky in 1989, and to the University Board of Trustees, and together they would give their final approval of a select candidate.

Carr told the *Herald-Leader* that he wanted "someone with leadership abilities, who works well with faculty and staff," someone "community oriented." And, continued Carr, "we are going to be looking for someone who wants LCC to work with business and industry." Meanwhile, Carr appointed University of Kentucky Community College System academic vice chancellor Anthony Newberry, former president of Ashland Community College, later president of Jefferson Community and Technical College in Louisville, as the interim LCC president. Tony Newberry's job in the Lexington Community College post was to "keep momentum going," while a new development officer, Betty McCann of Lexington, would explore perceptions held by Lexington area community leaders toward their local community college. Set to begin the fall 1993 semester, with record enrollment figures again predicted, Newberry soon reported that the fall start-up went "smoothly," in part because of the facilities

▲ Volunteers and adjunct faculty: left to right, Teresa Isaac, Linda Morgan, Betsy Byrne, and Brad Cowgill.

▶ Dr. Janice Nahra Friedel, president of Lexington Community College.

provided by the new Academic Technical Building. But Newberry also made it clear that there was no space to spare: "We must have set a record for the time it took from occupancy to bursting at the seams," Newberry told the *Herald-Leader*.

Enrollment at LCC doubled from 1986 to 1991 and gave rise to what had become a recurring discussion among interested parties of constructing a completely new LCC campus on UK's South Farm, 170 acres on the corners of Nicholasville Road and Man o' War Boulevard used for plant science research projects. A September 18, 1991, *Lexington Herald-Leader* article set the price tag for such a development at $13 million—probably an insufficient figure even at that point—and reported that UK President Wethington called a new campus for LCC "the second-highest priority at UK behind the construction of a new library." UK administrator Don Clapp said that LCC's growth was at such a pace that any South Farm facilities built for LCC would accommodate only part of the overflow. Unfortunately, the Kentucky state government in 1993 found itself immersed in a deep budget shortfall, and that precluded funding for anything so grand as an entirely new community college campus.

In the meantime, by December 3, 1993, the *Herald-Leader* reported the LCC presidential search committee had narrowed down the field to four candidates: Guy Altieri, vice president at Washtenaw Community College in Ann Arbor, Michigan; Donald Green, vice president for academic affairs at Genesee Community College, Batavia, New York; Clayton Johnson, president of Quincy College, Quincy, Massachusetts; and Janice Friedel, associate vice chancellor for academic affairs and planning for the Eastern Iowa Community College District in Davenport, Iowa. All candidates lined up well with their credentials, all were capable and experienced, and all seemed willing to take up the task.

A decision came on January 25, 1994, when the UK Board of Trustees announced that Janice Nahra Friedel, a graduate of the University of Iowa undergraduate, master's, and doctoral programs, would become president of Lexington Community College. Friedel had won fellowships from the Kellogg Foundation and another from the Institute in Women's History at Stanford University. Dr. Wethington told the January 26 *Herald-Leader* that Friedel brought "a wealth of experience in her work with community colleges and with education reform in the public schools." Ben Carr cited Friedel's extensive experience with "strategic planning, program development, continuing education" and noted that her "ideas" for LCC placed her ahead of the competition. Friedel, for her part, later told the *Herald-Leader* that she was convinced that she had made the right decision to come to LCC after informally talking over impressions of the school with local mall shop employees. "Many of them went to LCC and, without exception, their comments have been positive. They talked about the small classes, the quality of teaching."

In keeping with her predecessors' efforts, Friedel wanted to expand course and program offerings at LCC but realized early that "The challenge we face is not having the dollars to develop and deliver new programs," an observation her new faculty could have told her was something of a perpetual mantra, simply add faculty and staff salaries to the underfunded mix. "We need to explore ways we can financially support them," she observed, perhaps "through developing partnerships with businesses and other institutions in the area," although this was not a new idea. She hoped to see "a more aggressive approach" to winning federal and other grant dollars for upgrades in faculty development programs and new equipment for the College. But she also recognized that at LCC she was part of a very hierarchical system directed by the University of Kentucky, by this time one of only two such statewide arrangements in the country alongside the University of Hawaii.

One of the first things done was to scrap the old College newsletter and replace it with a much slicker and more detailed publication called *Lexington Community College Connections: A Newsletter for Faculty, Staff and Friends of Lexington Community College*. It was clearly the new "mouthpiece" of the College administration, often to the point where faculty criticized it for taking undue credit for activities and achievements with little connection to the new president. In the Summer 1994 issue, Friedel related that her "first three months as President of LCC will always be fondly remembered because of the warm welcome I received from the faculty, staff, students and community. I am impressed by the quality faculty and staff and their dedication to the college." To better strengthen her position, Friedel quickly moved to bring into her administration longtime insiders of the College, such as Dr. Anne Noffsinger, professor and coordinator of nursing, who became assistant to

the president and whose chief duties included college resource development and external relations.

Faculty continued to excel in bringing recognition and funding to the College. For example, the September 1994 newsletter announced that communications professor Cindy Leonard had brought in a $10,051 grant from the Department of Technical Education for a project entitled "Eliminating Gender Bias in Instruction at Lexington Community College." Mathematics professors Steve Ott and Lillie Crowley received funding from the National Science Foundation Instrumentation and Laboratory Improvement program for their project, "A Computer Algebra System for Calculus." The Disability Support Services program brought in a much-needed magnification system for the LCC library, thanks in part to assistance from the Lexington Lions Club Endowment Fund. Crowley also would work with Dr. Newberry and Darrell Abney of Maysville Community College on a three-year Advanced Technological Education project for the UK Community College System funded by the National Science Foundation.

Some LCC students were shining most brightly, too. For example, Bryan Johnson and Jonathan Watson, with UK students Sean Bryan and Ryan Meredith, were members of the *a cappella* quartet "IV," and were invited to perform at the national Christmas tree lighting ceremony at the White House on December 21, 1994. Three LCC nursing students, Charlotte Stewart, Ellen Hensley, and Tammy Anderson, won three of only four $500 scholarships awarded by the Kentucky League for Nursing.

In what was an unusual twist, two nontraditional students won the 1993 outstanding female and male graduate honors, Patricia Tucci and Sean McLaughlin, and shared a stage for the first time since their 1966 First Communion class at Lexington's Mary Queen of the Holy Rosary school, their story featured in the May 5, 1993, *Lexington Herald-Leader*. In the graduation ceremony the following year, LCC graduate Joyce Spears Beatty, a UK Minority Affairs administrator, was honored as the LCC Outstanding Alumnus during the May 1994 commencement ceremony. Graduation itself was an honor for those who achieved completion of their program of studies, and in 1994 that included 408 associate degrees granted, according to the June 15, 1994, *Lexington Herald-Leader*.

Division Chair Profile

Joanne M. Olson-Biglieri is beginning her first term as Division Chairperson of Social Sciences and Graphic Technologies after serving last year as Interim Chair. An Associate Professor of Spanish and French, she has coordinated these programs at LCC since 1988. Olson-Biglieri has an M.A. in Spanish Literature from Syracuse University and another in French Literature from Bowling Green State University of Ohio. Her B.A. is from SUNY, Oswego. She has studied abroad in France, Spain, Mexico, Quebec, and Italy. Olson-Biglieri brought years of full-time college teaching experience to LCC from schools such as Auburn University, Bowling Green State University and SUNY, Oswego.

Joanne Olson-Biglieri

While at LCC, she has focused on teaching and learning. This focus includes her work as a teaching consultant in the UKCCS Teaching Consultation Program and with the University of Kentucky's Professors for the Future Program. This year she was a recipient of the NISOD Excellence Award in Teaching from the University of Texas at Austin.

Olson-Biglieri's work with the community has involved teaching a course in advanced Spanish conversation, doing translations for various agencies like the Kentucky Department of Transportation and the Kentucky Ecuador Partners, and judging at high school language festivals. Currently, she facilitates for the New Century Lexington Strategic Planning sessions. Her institutional service includes serving on key college and system-wide committees such as the UKCCS Senate Program Development, Student Success and Retention, and International Education.

In her free time it is not unusual to find her on the tennis court (even at 6:30 a.m.)! She also enjoys travel, good food and theater.

◄ Faculty, staff, volunteers, and students frequently were profiled in the *LCC Connections* newsletter. Here, Spanish and French Professor Joanne Olson-Biglieri is the subject, Fall 1995.

▼ Graduation ceremonies were often held in UK's famed Memorial Coliseum, for many years home of the great University of Kentucky Wildcats men's basketball team.

▲ James Kolasa (left) with
Thomas Papanicolaou.

▶ Accounting Professor
Rasoul Taghizadeh.

For a number of years, Lexington Community College had attracted foreign students eager to study a variety of subjects in the College. The trend continued. LCC's admissions office processed students from all over the world, including students from such countries as Canada, Scotland, England, Ireland, the Netherlands, France, Germany, Russia, Bosnia, Hungary, Mexico, Bolivia, Peru, Guatemala, Egypt, Saudi Arabia, Iran, Iraq, Armenia, India, Nigeria, Kenya, Congo, Cameroon, Tanzania, Uganda, Ethiopia, South Africa, Kazakhstan, Kyrgyzstan, Indonesia, Malaysia, Japan, and the People's Republic of China, to name only a few among the many prominent countries represented. Students from these and other countries definitely gave LCC a cosmopolitan air that it would not have otherwise.

Students from these and other countries definitely gave LCC a cosmopolitan air that it would not have otherwise.

Student exchange programs were developed to allow students from Lexington Community College to experience an education overseas. Some examples of student exchange programs include that with the University of Wolverhampton, in the city and metropolitan borough of the same name in the West Midlands in England, and St. Patrick's College, Maynooth, in County Kildare, just west of Dublin, Ireland.

A still different sort of foreign program was added to the College for faculty interested in overseas travel and education. In 1995, sociology professor Dr. David Wachtel brought his years of experience to bear with a learning exchange program that linked LCC to Changsha College of Education in Hunan Province in the People's Republic of China. Chinese professors from Changsha University, Tianjin Normal University, and Tianjin Foreign Studies University would visit the LCC campus, and LCC professors would teach English to students in the Changsha College of Education. A dearth of College travel funds, especially for travel outside the United States, meant LCC faculty had to foot their own travel bill, but once in Changsha, the Chinese took care of the other expenses. Many faculty members made the

▲ Political Science Professor Tim Cantrell took his classes each semester to the state capitol in Frankfort to meet government officials. Here, Professor Cantrell and his class with Kentucky Governor Brereton Jones (front row, fourth from left).

trip as much for fun as for educational purposes. For the late English professor Dr. Arvin Jupin, it was about seeing the famed Great Wall of China, one of the seven modern wonders of the world. For geography professor Valiant Norman, it was not only about making friends, he told the February 2001 *LCC Courier*, "but also to be an example of what Americans can be, too." Many more faculty members would venture to other countries, including but not limited to Kenya, Spain, Italy, Greece, the United Kingdom, and France.

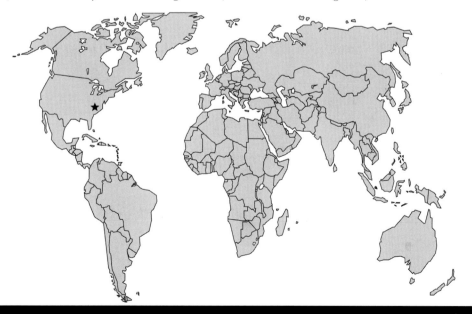

▼ English Professor Joy Famularo.

▼ Computer Science Professor Anas Anwar "Al" Sadat.

▼ Philosophy Professor Daniel Schuman.

▼ Building Maintenance staffer Mike Lahr.

▼ Sociology and Cultural Anthropology Professor Jeanne Humble.

▼ The ever-dependable Beverly Drake.

▼ Chemistry Professor Chad Mueller.

▼ Mathematics Professor Holly Pelphrey.

▼ English Professor John Scott.

▼ English Professor James Goode.

▼ Communications Professors Greg Feeney and Vicki Wilson.

Faculty & Staff

Lexington
Community College

Other reputed LCC "firsts" were recorded for fall 1995 in the *Connections* newsletter. In March, the slogan "LCC: Lexington's College of Choice" was adopted, a play on the school's acronym imminently preferable to that given it by some cheeky students, such as "Last Chance College." New programs continued to be proposed for the College, with one implemented in Environmental Science Technology. The LCC Alumni Association was established as an affiliate of the UK Alumni Association. Other international efforts were underway. The College established its Multicultural Affairs Office, with Burgin, Kentucky, native Denise White appointed as the first coordinator. Created too was a presence linking the College to the World Wide Web. The office for Institutional Research predated 1990, when Connie Christian served as the IR coordinator. That office was renamed Resource and External Affairs by Friedel's administration. Later, the name became Institutional Advancement and Research, first coordinated under that name by Sandra Green and then by Kelly Bevins.

Student Body President Meets Governor

While many LCC students were enjoying time off this summer, Student Body President Cathie Hill was taking their concerns straight to the Governor's Mansion.

Hill was the community college student representative when student body presidents met with Governor Brereton Jones in June.

"We expressed our concerns over rising tuition costs and funding for higher education and Governor Jones stated his thoughts on duplication of programs and new buildings for some of the community colleges," said Hill.

And those are just some of the challenges Hill is facing as LCC's new student body president. Low student involvement in the association continues to make the job of President a challenging one.

Cathie Hill, Student Body President

Nonetheless, she and Vice President Nathaniel Anderson have a few service projects already in the works. The two plan on spending a weekend making benches so students have more places to sit during Add/Drop. Hill said the benches will be scattered throughout campus during the year. Other ideas include a campus bookstore, establishing book/supply scholarships for students and volunteering at the Ronald McDonald House.

Taking on such an active role is nothing new for Hill, a second-year pre-pharmacy student. Long before her enrollment at LCC, she was a leader at Corbin High School and in her community. This summer, Hill volunteered as a youth and children's director at Corbin Central Baptist Church, organizing their day camp. She is also an outreach leader for Calvary Baptist Church in Lexington.

Hill topped off her busy summer at LCC by taking chemistry and making the Dean's List.

▲ Cathie Hill, president of the LCC Student Body, covered in the *LCC Connections* newsletter, Fall 1995.

Students continued their quest for recognition and their desire to make a difference in a variety of fields. For example, LCC Student Body President Cathie Hill of Corbin, Kentucky, was chosen to represent all of the state community colleges at a June 1995 meeting with Kentucky Governor Brereton Jones. Hill said that she "expressed our concerns over rising tuition costs and funding for higher education" to the governor. Another student who set an example was Thomas Franklin Schoenstra II of Louisa, Kentucky, in the Nuclear Medicine Technology program, who won a scholarship for $1,000 from the 1995 Health Scholars Program. A veteran assigned to aircraft carrier duty in the Desert Storm campaign of the 1990–91 Persian Gulf War, Schoenstra was just one of the many veterans to attend classes at LCC from all branches of the United States military.

◄ Miss LCC 1996 Chandra Barlow escorted by her father.

Unquestionably, there were many accomplishments made by the College during these years. Unfortunately, there were other actions that brought to light another side of the College administration. Perhaps as a sign of things to come, as early as 1995 things became heated when Dr. Friedel refused to make permanent the position of acting dean for academic affairs for Dr. Eunice Beatty, an LTI/LCC employee since 1978. Beatty was hired as acting dean in the first place because she had not completed the work for her doctorate. Her hiring was made with the understanding that once she finished her doctoral requirements she would become the permanent academic dean. But when that did not happen, Dr. Beatty, the highest-ranking African American in the LCC administration, sued the College and the University of Kentucky for racial discrimination and made it clear that she believed both UK and Community College System officials knew of "the endured circumstances of retaliatory and racist conduct directed at me by the LCC office of the president." The November 23, 1995, *Herald-Leader* article on the case reported that Beatty alleged "LCC and UK ignored her claims of racism," so she would seek punitive and compensatory damages for emotional distress, character assassination, and slander.

Perhaps even more difficult to explain was the May 12, 1997, resolution of censure against Dr. Friedel passed by the faculty of the College. The resolution stated that Dr. Friedel "knowingly misled the faculty" in the previous April 20 meeting regarding rule changes and their means of communication to the Community College System Chancellor. President Friedel "exhibited harassment, disrespect of and verbal abuse of faculty members," the resolution continued, and she "exhibited a pattern of authoritarian behavior" and inappropriately dismissed "the informed professional input of the faculty in regard to regulations, rule changes, division chair searches and recommendations of other committees." Thus, "The Faculty of Lexington Community College hereby censure Dr. Friedel and by a majority vote will declare our lack of confidence in her leadership."

Not everyone joined the LCC faculty in chastising Dr. Friedel. The LCC Advisory Board on May 13, 1997, voted "unanimously in favor of support" of the president and supported "her efforts to move the college forward. The vision, dedication, and leadership of Dr. Friedel has allowed LCC to move forward in many areas under adverse circumstances." They urged "all interested

▲ Ben Averitt in his counseling role.

citizens, faculty, and students to support LCC and Dr. Friedel as well as the Partners in Progress fund drive currently ongoing at the college. The Advisory Board," chaired by Richard Blanchard, who had been on the search committee that hired Friedel, "also endorses Dr. Carr's efforts at conflict mediation."

Whether this storm was the central impetus for what came seems unclear, but two months after the faculty censure resolution, Friedel was off to another job back in her native Iowa. In fact, it was a much better job than the LCC presidency, as head of the Iowa system of fifteen community colleges. "I have always had a strong interest in Iowa's educational system," she averred, adding that she took the new post because of the opportunities it presented, rather than simply to leave Kentucky. "Now is not the time to dwell on past problems," she said, "It is time for the college to consider its position within UK and focus itself on service to the community." Advisory chair Blanchard responded to her announcement with "Her departure is a loss to the state's educational system." President of the LCC Faculty Assembly, Professor Nolen Embry, told the *Herald-Leader* that he thought Friedel "was working to address the faculty's concerns," including sending a letter to faculty "promising to solve the problems." On the other hand, he added that her leaving would solve some of the problems.

▲ Psychology Professor Nolen Embry commands attention in class lecture.

▼ "LCC offers one of the most successful respiratory care programs (RCP) in the country." *Kentucky Kernel*, January 1997

Dr. Friedel, in parting, seemed intent to stay above the fray, at least publicly. "I believe the faculty, staff and community need to take great pride in the accomplishments of this college," she said, and added that "Community colleges are being called upon to do more for their states in terms of economic development, and I think LCC has tremendous potential to do that," reported the July 17, 1997, *Lexington Herald-Leader*. Whatever other subtexts might have been at play were silenced temporarily with her departure.

But the following year, Dr. Friedel sued her former employer for sex discrimination. Male presidents in the UK Community College System were paid more than she was, the suit alleged, and when Friedel raised objections, "her boss chided her for making waves," according to the suit. "Friedel finally decided to leave LCC rather than continue to work in a hostile environment," the April 9, 1998, *Herald-Leader* reported. Ironically, legal wrangling over alleged discrimination came to a close on another front, when the Lexington newspaper reported five days later that in the previous January UK had settled in its suit with Eunice Beatty.

ESTABLISHED 1894   UNIVERSITY OF KENTUCKY, LEXINGTON, KENTUCKY   INDEPENDENT SINCE 1971

For LCC students breathing is hard work

By Jenny Boggs
Contributing Writer

LCC's respiratory care program is breathing success.

Literally. The program, coordinated by Jim Matchuny, is one of six two-year medical programs where degree-seeking students may earn an associate degree in applied science. These programs are preparation for the state and national certification exams.

And prepare them it does. LCC offers one of the most successful respiratory care programs (RCP) in the country.

Kara Glass, a first-year student from Georgetown, Ky., said, "The program has its intense moments and requires a lot of studying."

LCC is well above the national pass average for both the Written Registered Respiratory Therapist Exam and the Certified Respiratory Therapy Technician Exam.

Matchuny attributes this success to faculty with excellent credentials, strong clinical affiliations with local hospitals and the support of LCC administration.

The RCP has a capacity of 48 students. Only 24 are accepted each year, though, with the average number of 30 students in the program.

The RCP has an excellent student-professor ratio. With three full-time faculty and a fluctuating number of part-time instructors relative to the size of the program, the ratio is better than 10-to-1.

Because of the "demanding and difficult program that requires serious adjustment in a student's personal schedule," Matchuny said, admission to the RCP is quite selective. Admissions personnel Christy Lancianese said students must have a 2.7 grade point average, an ACT score of 20 and usually some college experience.

After completion of the RCP, the benefits become overwhelmingly obvious to these hard-working students.

Four straight semesters of 70 credit hours reserved for physics, biology, anatomy, other sciences and clinicals prepare students for employment at hospitals, home health care, nursing homes and

physician's offices.

A starting base salary for a respiratory car practitioner is $11 to $12 an hour. LCC has a 100-percent job placement rate within the first six months of graduation. About 100,000 practitioners are employed today with an estimated need for 49,000 by the year 2005.

"Money Magazine's" fourth annual career survey ranks respiratory therapists 13th in the Top 50 fastest growing, most desirable jobs.

Aside from the financial security, Glass hopes her job will also be very fulfilling.

Respiratory care practitioners use their "technical and scientific skills to match a real need for human relations."

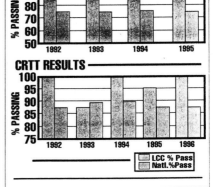

Lexington Community College
Respiratory Care Program
NBRC RESULTS & JOB PLACEMENT DATA
(12/96)

WRRT EXAM RESULTS

CRTT RESULTS

☐ LCC % Pass
☐ Natl.%Pass

CHRIS ROSENTHAL *Kernel staff*

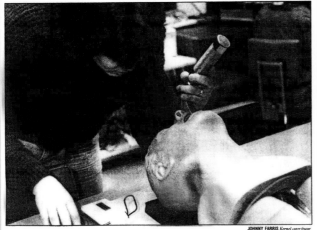

JOHNNY FARRIS *Kernel contributor*

CHAD THOMAS *Kernel staff*

BREATHE IN *Lisa Penn, left, a respiratory instructor demonstrates a procedure using a dummy. Respiratory therapy major Shawn Gannon connects tubing for a machine.*

Kentucky Kernel
Friday, January 31, 1997

While so many things seemed to change, however, other things stayed the same. Not the least of these was the growth of the College. The Winter 1997 *Connections* reported that LCC recorded a 5.3 percent increase in students since the year before, some 5,505 full-time students in 1996 over the 5,228 in 1995. Perhaps more impressive were the statistics for African American students, up 16 percent in 1996 from the year before. Dean of Student Affairs Paul Taylor pointed to two factors in explaining this growth: smaller class size that accommodated greater faculty interaction with students, and a tuition freeze from five years before that kept LCC tuition on a par with the other community colleges instead of with UK, as had been the case before. "With the tuition differential decision and the excellent faculty interaction with students, word is spreading that we are a very attractive educational package," Taylor said in *Connections*. By this time, LCC had 142 full-time faculty and 178 part-time faculty; it offered more than eight hundred courses, technical, semiprofessional, and pre-baccalaureate tracks of study, continuing education, professional development, and community service.

▼ LCC technical programs continued their well-established impressive records in the 1990s.

Program	Cycle of Review	Pass Rates on Licensure Exams	Graduation Rates	Employer Satisfaction	Alumni Satisfaction	Other Measures
Nursing	5 years (1994/1999)	94% 1st (5 yr. avg) 66% 2nd	5 yr. avg. 75 per year	High	High	External Accreditation/95% job placement
Nuclear Medicine	5 year (98/99)	90% 1st/98% 2nd attempt	5 yr. avg. 5 per year	High	High	Employment rate 85-100%
Dental Hygiene	7 year (96/97)	95% 1st/100% 2nd attempt	5 yr. avg. 20 per year	High	High	Employment rate 100%
Dental Laboratory Technology	5 year (98/99)	98%	5 yr. avg. 10 per year	High	High	ADA Comm. On Accreditation
Radiography	5 year (98/99)	'99 87%/'94-99 85%	'99 86% / '94-99 89%	IR	High	Alumni Survey Advisory Brd.
Respiratory Care	5 year (98/99)	88% (4 yr. avg.)	5 yr. avg. 16 per year	High	High	100% employment
Accounting Tech	5 year (96/97)	N/A				Program discont (8/99)
Architectural Tech	5 year (98/99)	N/A	5 yr. avg. 20 per year	High	High	
Business Tech	5 year (97/98)	N/A	About 40 per year		98.7% satisfied	Employment rate high
Computer Info Sys	5 year (99/00)	N/A	5 yr. avg. 30 per year	IR	IR	
Office Systems	5 year (97/98)	N/A	5 yr. avg. 13 per year	IR	IR	Employment rate high
Electrical Tech	5 year (96/97)	N/A	About 6 per year	High		All '99 grads hired bef. Grad.
Environmental Science Tech	5 year (98/99)	N/A	4 (in first grad. Class)			100% employed from 1st class

Table III-1: Technical Program Review Profile

University officials recognized that they needed to send in a seasoned veteran to manage LCC until yet another "permanent" president could be hired. They sent Dr. James Chapman, vice chancellor for public service and outreach for the Lexington Campus of the University. An Indianapolis native, Chapman had twenty-five years of service to the University under his belt, having started at Madisonville Community College as chief academic officer. Chancellor Carr said to the August 21, 1997, *Herald-Leader* that Chapman was "familiar with the university regulations and processes, and his knowledge and experience with community colleges will allow him to assist LCC during this important period."

▲ Dr. James Chapman, interim president of Lexington Community College. 2001UA028:0750, University of Kentucky Archives

Nineteen ninety-seven brought more far-reaching changes to the Kentucky higher education system, well beyond the teapot tempests at LCC. In May during a special legislative session, the Kentucky General Assembly passed the Postsecondary Education Improvement Act of 1997. Kentucky would replace the Council on Higher Education with the Council on Postsecondary Education to devise long-range plans and a statewide agenda for higher education. Six trust funds, administered by the aforementioned Council, would drive research, technological advancements, physical facilities and workforce developments, student financial aid, and an "excellence" fund for the regional universities. A Commonwealth Virtual University and a Kentucky Virtual Library, both again under Council supervision, would forward academic programs via the Internet, television, and other means. A Strategic Committee on Postsecondary Education (SCOPE) would advise the Council on Postsecondary Education on various educational matters.

But of far greater consequence to Lexington Community College and its sister community colleges was the change promised for the University of Kentucky Community College System. Fulfilling a long-held political goal by various state regional universities, the 1997 Kentucky Postsecondary Educational Improvement Act also created the Kentucky Community and Technical College Board to administer thirteen of the fourteen UK community colleges and twenty-five state technical schools, separating all but LCC from the control of the University of Kentucky. Other goals and objectives were declared in the legislation, House Bill 1, not the least being that by 2020 the University of Kentucky was to become a top twenty public research university.

◀ Dr. Jim Chapman was profiled in the *Kentucky Kernel*, UK's student newspaper, August 27, 1997.

Kentucky Kernel Welcome Back Edition, Wednesday, August 27, 1997

The new transitional man

Acting president to lead LCC

By Mat Herron
Campus Editor

New Lexington Community College President James Chapman knows what being in the minority feels like.

As one of 35 whites out of about 700,000 Indonesians on the island of Sumatra, Chapman had his picture taken in a natural history museum amid finger pointing and gawking from natives who had just lay their eyes on a rare specimen.

"It made you feel different," Chapman said, "and you shouldn't have to feel different.

"No matter who you are or what you do, the color of your skin affected how people treated you."

And no matter what administrative position he holds or what policies he implements, Chapman said he will do best for the students in the year of transition facing the lone community college to stick with UK.

Originally, from Indianapolis, Chapman served in the medical corps during the Vietnam War before becoming chief academic officer at Madisonville Community College in 1972.

Since then he has coordinated academic programs for freshman, served as assistant vice president for academic affairs, assistant chancellor for the Lexington Campus and most recently vice chancellor for public service and outreach, a position that has made him visible on and off campus.

Teaching classical mythology and medieval literature to undergraduates in the Honors Program reaffirms his commitment to educating young people, Chapman said.

"You almost get renewed every year as you deal with students," he said. "It helps you remember why you're here."

"Taking the campus off campus" with community outreach programs has been Chapman's primary duty as vice president of public service and outreach, and one he said he wants to continue after he takes the new position Sept. 1.

His goals include hiring more black faculty at LCC, helping minorities in areas like Bluegrass-Aspendale get a college education by providing transportation, using interactive cable or building a satellite campus, and putting a computer on the desk of every faculty member.

In this year before the new Kentucky Community and Technical College Board assumes control over the once-married 14 community colleges, strengthening the relationship between LCC and UK is, on the whole, Chapman's main objective — for a limited time only.

"I've got a year to capitalize on the strengths of LCC," he said.

"We need to see how the new organization is going to fall out, and how that's going to affect LCC. You just kind of go with that ... and try to capitalize on improving the relationship," he said.

Gaines Center Director Ray Betts said his friend of 20 years has been hungry for a position like this for some time.

"He's a remarkable individual, intelligent, diligent and dedicated," said Betts, who met Chapman when Chapman served as interim director for the Honors Program in the 1970s.

"He's the kind of person who's pinch-hit in many capacities."

> You almost get renewed every year as you deal with students. It helps you remember why you're here.
>
> ▼
> **James Chapman**
> *New acting president of LCC*

▲ Professor Robert Blake has fun with an engineering technology class.

▲ Vanessa Hughes (left) and Ethelene Denissoff show they have spirit.

It was not a popular decision among the majority in the University of Kentucky Community College System. In fact, none of the community colleges wanted a change in governance away from UK when it came down to it. "We actually polled students and faculty and advisory board members and others," UK President Dr. Charles Wethington said in an interview, "We polled the general public, and the numbers ranged from 66 to more than 90 percent against separation. The majority of Kentuckians didn't want to see this happen, didn't think this was a good idea. And yet the governor of Kentucky has a lot of political clout, if he or she determines to use it, and Governor [Paul] Patton determined to use it."

On January 23, 1998, President Wethington met with LCC faculty and staff to explain LCC's transition from administration under the Community College System to the University System, as well as to update faculty and staff on the College's presidential search. Wethington wanted the transition to be "seamless": "My goal," he said per the February 1998 *Connections*, "is that our students don't see a difference. It is important as we go into 1998 and beyond that what we have at LCC that

is good continues, that which we need to improve will be improved, and that our students will be served just as well or better" than before the change. Wethington supported the October 1997 LCC Transition Committee report that called for the College to maintain separate accreditation from the University, uphold its mission as a comprehensive community college, and guard its unique identity within the University. "We must look for some way to tie LCC in with the rest of the academic enterprise but still leave it with the kind of autonomy it needs to function," said Wethington.

Wethington acknowledged that the final word on the LCC direction came from the UK Board of Trustees, but he was optimistic:

> *The point is we have the flexibility to make it one of the best community colleges in the country, if it isn't already.... I think that, frankly, this provides an opportunity for us to do something first rate as a part of this comprehensive, statewide university. ...This is our opportunity to ensure that LCC continues to be something that shines.*

4
Celebration!

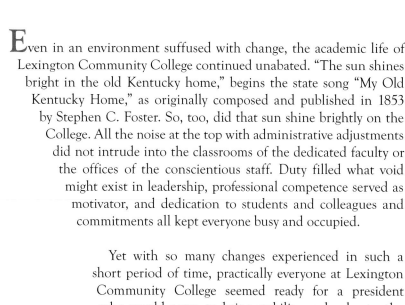

Even in an environment suffused with change, the academic life of Lexington Community College continued unabated. "The sun shines bright in the old Kentucky home," begins the state song "My Old Kentucky Home," as originally composed and published in 1853 by Stephen C. Foster. So, too, did that sun shine brightly on the College. All the noise at the top with administrative adjustments did not intrude into the classrooms of the dedicated faculty or the offices of the conscientious staff. Duty filled what void might exist in leadership, professional competence served as motivator, and dedication to students and colleagues and commitments all kept everyone busy and occupied.

Yet with so many changes experienced in such a short period of time, practically everyone at Lexington Community College seemed ready for a president who would serve to bring stability and calm to the school, someone who would work as a positive force, especially a positive force for the faculty, someone pleasant, personable, and friendly. As it happened, A. James Kerley fit the bill. Buoyant, cheerful to a fault, a virtual cheerleader for the school, Kerley was a welcome addition to the College.

According to Kerley himself and the *Lexington Herald-Leader,* he hailed from rural east Tennessee, attended the local schools, and afterward took a brief stab at a small business college in Knoxville. Nothing seemed to really catch his eye, however, so he left school and became eligible for the draft into the armed forces during the Vietnam War. Instead of leaving his assignment to the draft board, Kerley joined the United States Navy and

◀ Students straddle the UK-LCC sign next to the Moloney Building on Cooper Drive.

◀ Dr. A. James Kerley, president of Lexington Community College.

▼ Professor Erla Mowbray, nursing faculty.

Jim Kerley styled himself a "true believer" in the cause of the community college. He believed in the role and mission of community colleges, taking education to the people, making it available to anyone who wanted access to it, a true democracy of education. After graduate school, though, he first worked at Valdosta State College (now University) in Georgia, and then Union College in Barbourville, a school in the Appalachian Mountains in southeastern Kentucky, founded in 1874 and affiliated with the United Methodist Church, where Kerley was chair of the education department.

In 1986, Kerley applied for and received the post of dean of academic affairs at the University of Kentucky community college in Madisonville, the seat of Hopkins County. After a couple of years there, the presidency of UK's Hopkinsville Community College became open; Kerley applied and got the job, all of age thirty-eight. (So he moved from Hopkins County to Hopkinsville, county seat of Christian County, Kentucky, fitting in a fine Kentucky tradition separating seemingly sure partners in town and county names.) Kerley remembered Hopkinsville as "very southern," surrounded by large farms and host to a substantial African American population. Also there was a definite military flavor, thanks to the nearby U.S. Army facility at Fort Campbell. For nine years, Kerley lead Hopkinsville Community

served for two years. Among other things, it was during that time he met his wife Donna. Then after the navy, Kerley returned to Tennessee ready to apply himself to studies. He graduated from Tennessee Technological Institute with a bachelor's degree in social sciences and secondary education. Graduate work later included The Citadel for a master's and Florida State University for a doctorate in educational leadership.

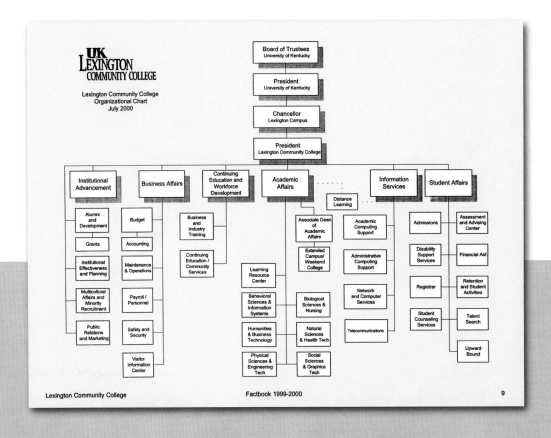

College, immersed himself in its local culture, helped raise his family, and learned all he could about college administration. In June 1998, Kerley made the jump from Hopkinsville to Lexington. It was a very different setting. Even so, Kerley thought it a "good fit," and so, too, did the UK Board of Trustees.

Taking up the post of president of UK's last community college might have proved daunting to some, but Kerley seemed to relish the spotlight. Many of the patterns of relationship between UK and LCC had been changed because of the forced separation of the other community colleges out from UK's watchful care. This meant a new definition of the UK-LCC relationship would have to be constructed. The year before, a Transition Committee co-chaired by Professors Michele Freed, Erla Mowbray, and Peggy Saunier prepared a report for Chancellor Ben Carr addressing these very points. The charge to the committee from Dr. Friedel was to "develop and facilitate the process for broad-based input to the discussion, analysis, and compilation of ideas and solutions posed by the challenges brought about by the structural changes to be implemented in compliance with the Postsecondary Education Improvement Act of 1997...." Those changes, ranging from college mission to accreditation issues to the educational programs and support services, now needed to be implemented. College leadership and administrative processes also were reevaluated.

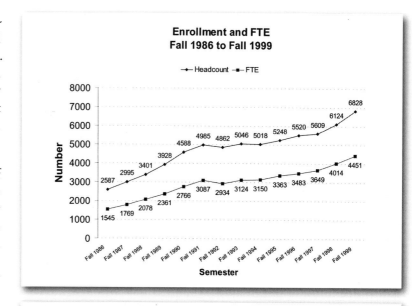

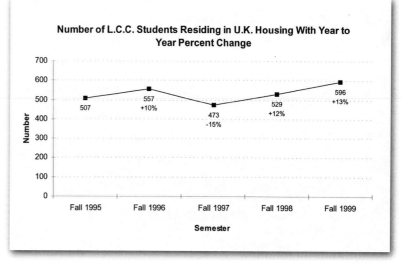

Mission & Values

Mission Statement

The University of Kentucky Lexington Community College provides open access to quality education for our diverse and growing community.

As an independently accredited community college, the University of Kentucky Lexington Community College offers:

- associate degree programs focused on career-oriented technical curricula and transferable prebaccalaureate curricula,
- programs and services supporting academic success,
- lifelong learning opportunities,
- economic and workforce development,
- an inclusive, student-centered environment, and
- a commitment to community service.

Vision

The University of Kentucky Lexington Community College will become one of the top twenty community colleges in the United States.

Values

We, at Lexington Community College, value

- the intellectual, professional, and personal growth of students, faculty, and staff;
- excellence in teaching, advising, and supporting students;
- student success through individualized attention;
- a climate of mutual respect and collaboration;
- an interactive and adaptive relationship with the community;
- open access to quality educational opportunities;
- lifelong learning;
- cultural diversity and human dignity;
- the continuous improvement of our programs and administrative processes;
- health, wellness, and safety within the College and community environments;
- innovation and efficiency in the use of resources; and
- personal and institutional accountability.

◀ "Girls' Night Out": Nursing faculty and College staff take in a Lexington Legends baseball game at Applebee's Park on North Broadway. From left: Lee Ann Walmsley, Lynn Roser, Jan Hicks, Phyllis Mulcahy, Vern Kennedy, and Erla Mowbray.

LCC's SIFE hits a home run for Legends baseball

BY TONY CORD
STAFF WRITER

Lexington is finally getting its own pro baseball team. The stadium is already under construction and the team's web site is up and running. The sale of Legends-related merchandise, however, could have been a different story.

The LCC chapter of SIFE – Students In Free Enterprise – will be pitching in to help open the fledgling team's store.

"This just happened to fall into our laps," said Virginia Fairchild, the head of the award-winning LCC- based SIFE team.

As it turns out, the original merchandiser pulled out at the last minute to take a more profitable offer. ▓▓ Brauer, of the Lexing-

ton Legends marketing staff and a former student of Fairchild's, stopped by and spoke to her abo▓

the store's difficulties. Seeing an opportunity for SIFE to help, she immediately offered to lend a hand.

When the Legends retail store opens in Turfland mall, several SIFE members and students in Fairchild's retail management class here at LCC will be there seeing how free enterprise works first hand while helping the store come into its own.

SIFE is a non-profit student organization interested in helping its members obtain experience with free enterprise, while teaching through example and community outreach programs. SIFE is open to all LCC students who wish to join. If you are interested, SIFE meets every Friday at noon in AT 102.

Interested in Lexington Legends Baseball? Visit the web site www.lexprobaseball.com.

UK News

▶ Article photo caption: Lexington Community College president James Kerley, right, talks with Gregory Bossé, a freshman from Haiti majoring in computer networking, in the lobby of the Oswald Building.

LCC adjusts to status as lone community college

CONTINUED FROM FRONT PAGE

considered is LCC's appeals board. While the rest of the University requires automatic course failure in cases of plagiarism or cheating, the community college allows more discretion. There also is the issue of ombud services. Should the LCC and UK ombuds operate independent of each other, or as part of the same office?

Working with UK

LCC is taking this time of change as an opportunity to strengthen connections between it and the rest of the University.

"We're just in the beginning stages, just beginning to think about what we can do," Kerley said.

Kerley has met with deans, chairs and professors, some of whom were making their first trip across Cooper Drive to LCC. He said he hopes to see, for example, the LCC architecture program working with the College of Architecture.

"My colleagues and I of the Lexington Campus look upon this more formal linkage with Lexington Community College as a splendid opportunity," Elisabeth Zinser, chancellor of the Lexington Campus, said. "It opens the door for innovative ways to prepare students for the transition to college, whether to LCC or the Lexington Campus. It invites creative thinking

about undergraduate research engagements for students at various levels of study. It prompts us to think more comprehensively about work force development for new business opportunities – coordinating the education of support professionals and technicians through LCC with the education of advanced practitioners and researchers through the University System."

With a stronger tie to the University, Lexington Community College officials also see themselves as having a role to play in UK's goal of becoming a top 20 public institution.

"The missions of the two institutions are different, but they compliment each other," said Teresa Arnold, LCC's director of public relations. "On a national level, you're seeing many community colleges being noted as top educational entities, and there's no reason LCC can't be seen that way."

The community college also has the role of bringing good students to UK who might need a community college at first. Many LCC graduates successfully continue or add onto their community college degrees at UK.

"We take students wherever they are and work with them," Kerley said.

— DOUG TATTERSHALL

'UK's community college' enjoying single life

• **Lexington Community College has become a unique entity in the state.**

Sometimes leaving things unchanged causes change. That has been the case with Lexington Community College, which was not separated from the University under the state's higher education reform, as were the state's 13 other community colleges.

To begin with, there is the change in enrollment. LCC set a new record this fall with 6,110 students, an increase of 9.38 percent over last academic year. That number includes students from 108 Kentucky counties, 36 U.S. states and 23 foreign countries. LCC President Jim Kerley – himself one of the changes at LCC, having

come from Hopkinsville Community College – credits the record enrollment in part to higher education reform, which left LCC as the only community college under UK's administration.

"We are more integrated with the University than ever before," he said. "It sets us apart from the other 13 colleges."

Because of that, LCC now bills itself as "UK's community college."

Chain of command

LCC's unchanged status also is causing changes in administration. No longer reporting to a community college chancellor, the college also does not answer to the Kentucky Community and Technical College System as the state's 13 other community col-

leges do. The result is in some cases more autonomy and in some cases new people to answer to. A University Senate Council task force is reviewing all of LCC's rules. In some cases, the council will change rules, while in the case of administrative rules, it will make recommendations to President Charles T. Wethington Jr., who will submit changes to the Board of Trustees.

"That doesn't mean that LCC will have to change. It's a two-way street. There may be changes that the rest of the University wants to make," said Roy Moore, chair of the University Senate, which now includes nine new members from LCC.

An example of changes being

SEE LCC, BACK PAGE

LCC becomes UK's lone community college.

Clearly, there was need for reevaluation. One of the peculiarities of the UK-LCC relationship involved the "separateness" of LCC within UK. Students found some of the strange, albeit long-in-place, nuances of the relationship especially annoying. For example, students who wanted to attend UK *and* LCC simultaneously had to submit separate applications. A more frustrating problem still lay in store for the student who took classes at UK and LCC, taken together making for a full-time schedule, only to discover that one was not considered full-time at either school. This became a real issue for the avid UK sports fan who hoped to secure precious UK sports event tickets, especially basketball and football tickets. One student caught in this net, Jon Rasmussen, wrote to the *LCC Courier* to ask, "Is LCC part of UK or not?" And while tickets might be hard to get for a time, LCC students did already share housing, library, and exercise facilities with the rest of the UK student body.

Faculty concerns usually turned on different issues. It rarely became serious, but the faculty was long known to raise its voice in protest of policies, procedures, or even over basic treatment. Culture clash sometimes occurred between UK and LCC faculty and staff, too. Sometimes certain UK faculty members pointed to students at the University who might otherwise not be admitted, using the LCC open admissions policy as a "back door" into the University and its selective admissions. Sometimes certain LCC faculty members voiced disparaging opinions of UK faculty for their academic snobbery toward the community college, their lack of understanding of the mission and goals of a community college, and, in certain instances, reputedly poor classroom teaching because of their heavy, and preferred, research commitments. One might hope, if caught in one of these arguments, that a consensus could be reached that it was a comparison of apples and oranges, and all stood under the same UK umbrella.

One complaint hit much closer to home, even literally so. Faculty salaries at LCC remained low to the point of insult. The College not only fell behind its benchmark institutions on faculty compensation, Kentucky fell at the bottom of the southern schools, and southern schools were at the bottom in the country. The June 20, 2003, *Lexington Herald-Leader* reported the average salary of a tenured associate professor at $40,000. Duties included a five-course-per-semester teaching load, student advising and scheduling, com-

mittee assignments, College and divisional meetings, professional development activities, and community service work. It was a schedule that could wear down the young and strong, and the financial "reward" was almost a joke, especially when one considers Lexington is one of the most expensive towns in Kentucky to live in. According to the 2000 *Institutional Self-Study*, when compared to the eight benchmark institutions, LCC salaries fared poorly: fifth out of eight for professors,

▲ Outstanding speakers often are brought to campus. Here, the Rev. Reed Polk makes his presentation during Faculty-Staff Development Day, August 1998.

▲ Mathematics Professor Paul Blankenship visits with UK Agricultural Economics Professor Loys Mather.

eighth out of eight for associate professors, tied for fifth and sixth out of seven for assistant professors, and third out of five for instructors. Even more depressing were the figures for adjunct faculty compensation, a group exploited nationally. While the College "did increase the starting salary for all [full-time] faculty positions to $30,000 in 1999," and brought all lower salaries to that level, the *Self-Study* noted that "At every rank faculty salaries continue to remain below the national average. Meeting the national average would require a significant increase for each rank—10.4 percent for professors, 19.4 percent for associate professors, 19.1 percent for assistant professors, and 12.8 percent for instructors."

On a more positive note, one new short-term program became available at LCC. A new partnership developed between LCC, Central Kentucky Technical College in Lexington, and Maysville Community College. All three teamed up with the massive Toyota

▲ Architectural Technology open house in 1997 was a nice venue for Professor Lillian Fallon Graetz (left).

Motor Manufacturing facility in Georgetown, Kentucky. Toyota employed thousands in central Kentucky at the facility and paid them well for their labor. In addition to their commitment to quality, Toyota looked for opportunities for innovation. The company identified a need for what were being called Multi-Skilled Maintenance workers. Something of a manufacturer's hybrid, these workers were to have skills in various electronics, digital circuits, mechanical fabrication, and in other areas, according to the October 2000 *LCC Courier*. To train these workers, Toyota partnered with LCC, Central Kentucky Tech, and Maysville and developed a two-year associate's program where, upon completion, a graduate could earn from $35,000 to $45,000 right out of college. LCC engineering professor Mike Binzer summed it up rather nicely: "Great opportunities and great pay."

April 2001

Civil engineering program back by popular demand

BY LANCE SOUTHWORTH
ASSISTANT EDITOR

Back before a lot of us ever thought about going to college, LCC was named The Lexington Technical Institute. This institute offered a civil engineering associate degree that trained students to have the basic knowledge to equip them to help engineers without all of the unnecessary extras.

Now, after many years of high demand for techs, the local civil engineering firms, along with UK and LCC, have formed a committee to bring forth a curriculum that will ship out two-year engineer technicians.

Cyndy Carroll, the LCC professor in charge of forming and overseeing this course, usually teaches mechanical engineering but said she "somehow fell into the job of running this!"

LCC will be the only school in the state offering this Associate of Applied Science degree starting this fall. This Civil Engineering Technology Program will train the students in fields of concentration leading to career options in commercial, residential and highway surveying; highway construction management; construction estimation; construction documentation; construction site design and wastewater management.

John Slugantz, project manager for the local firm GRW Engineers, Inc., graduated from LTI back in '84 before the tech program was discontinued.

"Knowledge and application wise, it is the same as UK," says Slugantz referring to the ability of this new program. The program at UK is calculus-based; LCC's program will be trigonometry-based.

GRW has been credited with the engineering of sites like: The Lexington Legends Stadium, Tates Creek and Palomar Centers, RiteAide sites all over the country, and the McCreary County Federal Prison. The mechanical engineers at GRW were responsible for the upgrade of UK Commonwealth Stadium.

Slugantz mentioned with that the high drop-out rate at UK in the Civil Engineering Program, this gives students a different avenue.

"Fifty percent to 60 percent of the freshmen drop out within the first year, and 10 percent to 15 percent of transfer students to UK drop out," according to Dr. George Blandford, director of undergraduates in civil engineering.

Only students with a four-year degree from UK can become a registered engineer in the state of Kentucky. But the tech program can be a step up the ladder.

"This is a good place for students to get their feet wet," stated Blandford.

GRW is in need for civil techs in a bad way. Over the years, since the tech program was dismissed, only engineers have been coming out into the work force and having to do techs' work. According to the U.S Department of Labor, expectations for engineer technician employment is projected to increase 10 percent to 20 percent overall through 2008.

Think being a technician won't pay off? Think again. Base salary, depending on experience and schooling, runs between $25 and $30 thousand. Pay can be higher depending on the demand in that area and the local pay scale.

For more information on the Civil Engineer Technician Program starting this fall, you can contact Cyndy Carroll at 257-4872, ext. 4111 or in MB 143.

◄ Professor Mike Binzer teaches Electrical Engineering Technology.

New programs brought additional students to LCC, placing additional strain on already stretched facilities. In the fall of 1998, the school set yet another enrollment record, over 6,100 students, a 9.75 percent increase over the previous year. Especially encouraging was the growing diversity of the student population. According to the October 1998 *Connections*, since fall 1997, enrollments were up approximately 25 percent among African Americans, 22 percent among Asians and Pacific Islanders, 20 percent for American Indians, and 16 percent for Hispanics. "LCC is seeing the rewards of a combination of several factors," said Kerley, "including public awareness of the excellent level of teaching and student services we provide, and our commitment to cultural diversity.... We feel that a great part of our growth this year is due to the fact that students recognize the importance of having a degree from the University of Kentucky. LCC is the only community college to remain with UK," Kerley observed, "so we can continue to offer students many benefits because of that relationship. We are proud to be part of UK."

By the fall of 2000, more than seven thousand students attended LCC. Space again was a serious issue. Some relief came when Assistant Dean for Academic Affairs Tri Roberts informed the school newspaper that the College had leased the former Sullivan College building on Regency Road in south Lexington to alleviate the crunch on the Cooper Drive Campus. Non-credit courses already offered would continue at the East Campus facility on Lexington's Winchester Road. The new South Campus on Regency Road could accommodate between 300 and 350 students immediately and perhaps more later.

Enrollment by Program
Fall 1995 to Fall 1999

	Fall 1995 # Enrolled	Fall 1996 # Enrolled	Fall 1996 1 Year % Change	Fall 1997 # Enrolled	Fall 1997 1 Year % Change	Fall 1998 # Enrolled	Fall 1998 1 Year % Change	Fall 1999 # Enrolled	Fall 1999 1 Year % Change	5 Yr % Change
Technical Programs										
Accounting	84	74	-12%	72	-3%	71	-1%	0	-100%	-100%
Architecture	102	100	-2%	100	0%	98	-2%	125	28%	23%
Business	211	238	13%	252	6%	254	1%	294	16%	39%
Computer Info. System	172	189	10%	230	22%	274	19%	381	39%	122%
Dental Hygiene	46	46	0%	45	-2%	47	4%	47	0%	2%
Dental Lab	29	32	10%	27	-16%	22	-19%	23	5%	-21%
Elec-Enginerring	63	69	10%	59	-14%	46	-22%	48	4%	-24%
Environmental Science	0	11	100%	40	264%	52	30%	43	-17%	*258%
Mech-Engineering	7	4	-43%	0	-100%	n/a	n/a	n/a	n/a	n/a
Nuclear Medicine	11	10	-9%	9	-10%	11	22%	12	9%	9%
Nursing	179	184	3%	177	-4%	185	5%	196	6%	9%
Office Administration	92	91	-1%	69	-24%	76	10%	70	-8%	-24%
Pre-Health Majors	640	562	-12%	555	-1%	569	3%	539	-5%	-16%
Radiography	51	49	-4%	85	73%	64	-25%	53	-17%	4%
Real Estate**	7	3	-57%	0	**	**	**	**	**	**
Respiratory Care	45	39	-13%	31	-21%	28	-10%	14	-50%	-69%
Technical Prog Total	**1739**	**1701**	**-2%**	**1751**	**3%**	**1797**	**3%**	**1845**	**3%**	**6%**
Transfer Programs										
AA/AS	4	2	-50%	0	-100%	9	100%	11	22%	175%
Pre-Bacc	1908	2037	7%	2091	3%	2280	9%	2467	8%	29%
Transfer Prog Total	**1912**	**2039**	**7%**	**2091**	**3%**	**2289**	**9%**	**2478**	**8%**	**30%**
Undecided										
2-YR Undecided	330	360	9%	390	8%	508	30%	614	21%	86%
4-YR Undecided	898	936	4%	956	2%	1025	7%	1279	25%	42%
Non-Degree	349	464	33%	370	-20%	499	35%	612	23%	75%
Undecided Total	**1577**	**1760**	**12%**	**1716**	**-3%**	**2032**	**18%**	**2505**	**23%**	**59%**
Grand Total	**5228**	**5500**	**5%**	**5558**	**1%**	**6118**	**10%**	**6828**	**12%**	**31%**

* 4 Year Percent Change
** Program became Business Technology Option.

South Campus relieves growing pains

BY FERRAN ROBINSON
CO-EDITOR

It's a familiar scenario: It's registration time and that 11 a.m. class that fits so perfectly into your schedule is closed. So what do you do?

The answer is to register for that elusive class at LCC's new South Campus. At least that's what LCC officials hope.

Beginning Oct. 1, LCC will begin moving into a new campus at the former Sullivan College on Regency Road. Students currently enrolled in general education courses at LCC's East Campus will be the first to experience the offerings of the new facility when their classes move there beginning Oct. 16.

Tri Roberts, Assistant Dean of Academic Affairs, said the decision to move to the new campus, which is

Photo by Ferran Robinson
The South Campus will take over the former Sullivan College building on Regency Road.

under a three-year lease, was a result of limited space at LCC due to a continually growing enrollment. The East Campus, also leased, will continue to host non-credit courses.

When spring 2001 registration begins, all new and returning students will have the opportunity to attend classes at the South Campus. According to Roberts, the South Campus will offer many general education classes that are familiar to students. Nineteen full-time faculty members will be on board at the new facility.

Of the amenities offered at the campus, Roberts said "It'll be an opportunity for students to go to a site and do everything at that site." He said the campus offerings will include registration, counseling, a bookstore, a computer lab with internet access, a lounge area and vending. The school hopes these features, as well as the campus's location, will be a draw for students who often have a hard time getting the classes they want at the times they want.

According to Roberts, South Campus can handle an enrollment of 300-350 students initially. LCC currently has about 7,200 students. LCC

See **SOUTH CAMPUS** pg. 4

◀ South Campus blooms.

Another site that offered possible relief from the nagging classroom space issue was to create a presence in downtown Lexington. Mayor Pam Miller certainly liked the idea, as did Lexington economic development director Bob Drakeford. Even the chair of the Kentucky Council on Postsecondary Education, Gordon Davies, weighed in on the subject and gave it his blessing. In an editorial response in the July 30, 2001, *Lexington Herald-Leader*, Dr. Kerley styled these proposals as "encouraging." Both downtown and LCC could benefit. A new building for Cooper Campus remained the top priority to address this issue, Kerley reiterated, but there was no aversion to classes offered downtown. "The cornerstone of LCC's mission is access," wrote Kerley. "By eliminating barriers to education, whether related to finances, transportation, or scheduling, true open access becomes a reality." Models existed for such ventures in Ann Arbor, Michigan, and in Portland, Oregon, where the community colleges there "have well-equipped main campuses complemented by branch campuses that serve special populations." LCC might gladly follow such successful models.

All talk of a new site for Lexington Community College after 2001 would have to await the word of a new president at the University of Kentucky. The University Board of Trustees had decided in 1999 to set Dr. Wethington's contract as president of the University to expire on June 30, 2001. He would continue to work for the University for two years after that as a fund-raiser. In the meantime, the University was determined to seek out a president to raise UK to new heights: UK as a top-twenty public research university in the United States. The man they chose to lead this highly ambitious endeavor was Lee T. Todd, a native of Earlington, a small community in Hopkins County, Kentucky. Dr. Todd was a 1968 UK graduate in electrical engineering. He earned his master's in 1970 and his doctorate in 1973 at the Massachusetts Institute of Technology. In 1974, Dr. Todd returned to UK as a professor of electrical engineer-

Enrollment by Kentucky County
Fall 1999

Lexington Community College
Factbook 1999-2000

NEWS RELEASE

Cooper Drive, Lexington, KY 40506-0235

FOR IMMEDIATE RELEASE
MEDIA CONTACT: Vernal Kennedy, Director of Public Relations and Marketing
(859) 257-4872 Ext. 4189

LCC is fifth fastest growing two-year college in nation

LEXINGTON, KY (December 11, 2001) – Lexington Community College ranks fifth on the list of the nation's top 50 fastest growing public two-year colleges with enrollments between 5,000 and 9,999 students, according to a report in the December 10 issue of *Community College Week*. The report utilizes data from the National Center for Education Statistics, a branch of the U.S. Department of Education, to rank the colleges that experienced the largest percentage change in total student enrollment between fall 1994 and fall 1999. During that time, LCC experienced 36 percent growth.

"This ranking simply confirms what we've known for a long time," says LCC president Dr. Jim Kerley. "Lexington Community College is increasingly becoming the first choice for more and more students. Some of our incredible growth can certainly be attributed to changing workforce demands, but I also like to think that our quality faculty, small class sizes, flexible scheduling options and warm environment have contributed to our success."

The College's enrollment continues to climb with the unofficial fall 2001 figure of 7,903 students reflecting a 9.6 percent increase over fall 2000.

ing, where he won several teaching awards, including the UK Alumni Association Great Teacher Award. In 1983, Dr. Todd left UK to work for a company he founded in 1973, DataBeam Corporation, "the world's leading provider of real-time collaboration and real-time distance learning software and development platforms." In 1998, he sold DataBeam to IBM. Todd worked as a senior vice president at IBM until 2001, when he left to become the president of the University of Kentucky, effective on July 1 of that year.

> "The cornerstone of LCC's mission is access. By eliminating barriers to education, whether related to finances, transportation, or scheduling, true open access becomes a reality."

In one of his first acts to involve LCC, the new UK president sought to address the lingering issue of establishing a downtown campus, including an administrative presence and regular course offerings. Dr. Todd announced in the March 1, 2002, *Herald-Leader* that a lease had secured use of space in the Kentucky Utilities building downtown between Main and Vine streets. The objective was to "relocate" LCC students and perhaps find new ones with a downtown location. According to the same article, UK also would offer courses there. LCC classes would include such topics as business, customer service, and theater. Later, perhaps, courses in history, psychology, and engineering might be offered. From 150 to 200 students were anticipated for the initial courses scheduled. Unfortunately, it never worked. After a year, the LCC course offerings were discontinued. UK never offered classes there. The LCC Continuing Education office, along with several UK administrative offices, remained on location downtown as a reminder of the effort.

Another campus, long in the works, opened on January 16, 2002, in Winchester, Clark County, Kentucky. Winchester elected officials had approved renovation of the College Park Library building, providing $200,000 for that purpose. After ten years of offering classes in several Clark County locations, now classes, registration, and advising could center on one single place. The new campus featured four classrooms, a student lounge, and staff workstations, according to the January 17, 2002, *Herald-Leader*. Eventually, LCC wanted to offer degrees from start to finish from the Winchester-Clark County campus. Students from Winchester and Clark County could earn an LCC associate's degree without leaving home.

Other novel plans addressed the campus crowding issue. To add to summer sessions, "Weekend College" brought classes to campus, even on Sunday. Later, Fall and Spring II sessions were offered, literally building a semester within a semester, to allow for still more student accommodation.

Students could hone their academic recall skills by joining the long-established LCC Academic Team. Academic tournaments usually involved six rounds of competition with questions formulated to test areas ranging from general knowledge to the humanities, mathematics, and natural and social sciences. The LCC team competed with four-year institutions as well as other community colleges. One mix of competition included Ohio University, Georgetown College, Transylvania University, and Louisville's Jefferson Community College. LCC teams over the years faired very well against such solid competition, frequently winning tournaments. Advisors Vicki Partin and Larry Mullins, both mathematics professors, had every right to be proud of their team's accomplishments.

{ **[ROTC] is a relaxed atmosphere, heavy on camaraderie,... where confidence, teamwork, and leadership are the prevailing ideals.** }

Academic team wins tourney at home

BY FERRAN ROBINSON
CO-EDITOR

The LCC Academic Team won the second tournament of the semester on October 14 with a clean sweep of the competition in front of a home crowd.

The six-member team is comprised of LCC students James Hall, Rick Hayes, Robert Murray, Rebel Solomon, Barret Webb and Dan Whittaker.

LCC placed first in the tournament with 195 points. EKU was second with a score of 185. Georgetown College took third with 183 points. Ohio University and Jefferson Community College Southwest finished fourth and fifth, respectively.

Four academic tournaments are held each semester. The team

Photo by David Hardy

The LCC Academic Team faces off against Transy in the second round of the October 14 tournament.

tied for second in the previous tournament at Georgetown College. After a tie-breaking round,

the team took home a third place trophy.

The Academic Team's mem-

bers are part of a club that any LCC student can join. The club's faculty coaches are Vicki Partin, Larry Mullins, and Val Norman.

An academic tournament typically involves six rounds of competition. There are two halves to each round with 20 toss-up questions per half. The questions come from 5 categories: mathematics, natural science, humanities, social sciences and general knowledge.

The LCC team belongs to a 16-team league made up of 14 Kentucky schools and 2 schools from Ohio. LCC is in division II of the league.

The next league tournament will be held at Pikeville Community College on November 18 where LCC will defend its first-place status.

ROTC program now open to LCC students; offers chance to practice teamwork, self-confidence

BY REID HURLEY
EDITOR

The media-driven world in which we live often blurs the line between reality, television and movies. They've given us a picture of the army as testosterone -driven men with chips on their shoulder. Not so with the University of Kentucky Army ROTC program.

Drill-sergeants won't be screaming degrading obscenity laced tirades at cadets, and officers won't be yelling, "drop and give me fifty." in the halls and buildings occupied by the ROTC. It is an relaxed atmosphere, heavy on camaraderie , an atmosphere where confidence, teamwork and leadership are the prevailing ideals.

The ROTC program is open to all students attending UK or LCC. Cadet John Plymire enrolled in ROTC to earn a scholarship after his first year in law school. After school Plymire will be part of the National Guard, with hopes of earning a spot on the Judge Advocacy Group (JAG). JAG is responsible for handling legal matters for all military personnel, in civilian or military court.

A common misconception about ROTC is that cadets have to serve active duty in the military upon completion of college. This is only partly true. If you leave the program prior to your

> The ROTC requires dedication in the classroom, where military history, map reading and other skills required for a person entering a military life are taught.

junior year, provided you have not yet signed a contract or accepted a scholarship, you have no future responsibility to the military. Furthermore, many Army ROTC graduates choose to go on to the National Guard or Army Reserves. No matter where you serve your post-graduation time, you will do so as a commissioned officer.

LCC sophomore Joe Henderson has been part of the ROTC since high school, where he was enrolled in the junior ROTC. Henderson is a member of the Kentucky National Guard. He says that most material in the program to this point has been a review, attributable to him already being in the service.

On why he enrolled in ROTC, Henderson says, "(ROTC)...Gives good leadership and good discipline, which was something that I needed at the time...plus the tuition wasn't bad."

ROTC, from the beginning, will take up more personal time than the average class. There are summer camps, as well as weekend training exercises which can take one day or the whole weekend. Whether or not the weekend trips are voluntary depends on how far along in the program a student is.

On March 3 the ROTC had a

Photos by Reid Hurley

Cadet John Plymire said he enrolled in ROTC to earn a scholarship after his first year of law school. He plans to continue with the program and to become involved with JAG.

Cadets spend much of their time on retreat performing challenging drills. While such activities are voluntary, peer pressure does cause most cadets to participate.

one-day training exercise in eastern Kentucky. They met at Barker Hall on the UK campus at 5 a.m. From there they split into groups, and drove to meet the Blackhawk helicopters that transported the separate groups to the area where they would be training for the day.

Throughout the day the cadets, staying in smaller groups, rotated through three exercises.

The groups would begin in the Engagement Skills Trainer, (EST). The EST is located inside a large room, at the back of which is a room with large windows looking in. Inside the room are four large screens measuring about 10 ft. by 8 ft. Twenty feet in front of the screens is a line of rifles and pistols commonly used by the military.

The guns have the same weight and recoil but are equipped with lasers that are picked up on the screens to record "kills," and "hits." Projectors situated directly in front of the cadets project different scenarios on the screen -- ranging from a hostage situation in what looks like a run-down South

American town, to an ambush in some far away East Asian jungle. At the end of each situation the cadets are told how many "kills," or "hits" they have.

The next exercise was the rappelling tower. Standing at forty feet, the tower can be an intimidating site for a person new to rappelling.

To rappel you tie a rope around your waste and crotch area in a series of complicated knots, making what is called a Swiss harness, (mountain climbers and people rappelling for fun usually use a store bought harness commonly made out of nylon). You then attach yourself to the rope using a D-ring, (a piece of mountaineering equipment that is a thick metal oval with a clip on one side). Put your toes on the very edge of the tower, lean back as far as you can and step back into nothingness. For a first-timer that step can be very nerve-racking. The purpose of the

See ROTC, page 15

▲ Famed journalist Helen Thomas, a Winchester, Kentucky, native, addressed the May 2003 commencement for LCC graduates. Thomas accompanied by Professor Tim Cantrell.

◀ Political Science Professor Hossein Motamedi enjoys a day at Keeneland Race Track. Motamedi took over the duties for the LCC political poll from Tim Cantrell following Cantrell's retirement. The LCC political poll was much anticipated in local political races because of its solid record for accuracy.

▼ Tim Cantrell stopped to chat with former LCC student and State Representative Susan Westrom (D-Fayette). The smiles convey the participants' level of excitement over the activities at the 2000 Democratic National Convention.

October 2000   *News*   **Page 7**

Professor introduces LCC to the DNC

BY THERESA STANLEY
CO-EDITOR

LCC Political Science Professor Tim Cantrell participated in the 2000 Democratic National Convention, in Los Angeles. As a Kentucky delegate, he received a ground-floor view of the activities.

Spectators will remember the overwhelming excitement of Al Gore as he stepped up to the platform to deliver the speech of his lifetime. He pulled Tipper close to him and planted a kiss never before seen from the man who is fighting the ghost of scandalous Bill Clinton.

According to Cantrell, "…it is a natural thing to do…I would do the same thing."

Cantrell says the delegates inside were oblivious to the daily demonstrations and chaos of protesters, which included a Rage Against the Machine concert.

Cantrell has been a state delegate in past years but this year was elected by his party to represent our state at the national level on the ground floor of the four-day convention. While on the floor, Cantrell ran into a former LCC student, Susan Westrom, who is now a Kentucky Democratic Representative from Fayette County.

Cantrell, his wife and other delegates spent five days with Ky. Governor Paul Patton and his wife. They visited the California Yacht Club, Sony Studios and Hollywood Race Course.

Cantrell gained a wonderful experience of great food, fun and fellowship while the rest of the television viewing audience received flashes of pandemonium and locked lips.

For more information on Cantrell's trip, he can be contacted at Tacant00@pop.uky.edu.

Democrats know how to party

Tim Cantrell stopped to chat with former LCC student and State Representative Susan Westrom (D-Fayette). The smiles convey the participants' level of excitement over the activities at the 2000 Democratic National Convention.

Photo submitted

Spring Fling has global flair

BY BRIAN QUINN
STAFF REPORTER

The third year of LCC's Spring Fling is bringing a bit of international flavor to campus. On April 18 from noon to three in the afternoon, 14 student organizations with the help of LCC faculty will put on an event to help bring the LCC community together outside the classroom setting. The event will be held outside in the courtyard area with free food, drinks, music, entertainment, leis and prizes.

Aside from the traditional hot dogs and hamburgers, this year there will be a small display of ethnic foods. Local eateries including Oasis, Kashmir, Marikka's and The Great Wall will donate samples of their traditional ethnic foods.

In keeping with the international theme, there will be a group of belly dancers from Mecca dance studio performing with live drummers. Along with the drummers, there will be a salsa band and steel drum band performing live as well. There will also be a demonstration of Capioera, a mixture of African and Brazilian martial arts, by Steven Harris.

The student organizations involved will be running booths with cotton candy, popcorn and the Coup de Gras funnel cake. Also, the Student Government Association will be holding elections for all offices, with drawings for prizes for students who vote.

Erica Caton, the faculty planner for Spring Fling, said the college wanted to bring the students, faculty members and alumnae together to interact outside the classroom environment and have fun. Caton went on to say she would like to see everyone participate, as long as they weren't missing class.

On Friday April 20, there will be an Appalachian Heritage Festival outside the AT building with traditional food and music by Homer Ledford.

◄ Spring fling enjoyed by all: free food, free beverages, and free entertainment.

▼ Flags from many countries brought an international flavor to the Oswald Building lobby.

ESL sparks conversation

BY CATHERINE NG
ASSISTANT EDITOR

Have you ever stammered in the presence of your classmates and professors because English is not your native language? Or scratched your head while trying to write your English essay? Do not hesitate, the English as a Second Language class (ESL) is what you need.

LCC is providing a program for international students who need to improve their proficiency in English. At the beginning of spring semester 2001, a few LCC faculty members decided to offer an ESL class. It is offered by the LCC International Affairs Action Team to help students from different countries gain confidence in speaking English. ESL at LCC is informal, and it is neither a grammar class nor a writing class.

"The goal of offering an ESL class at LCC is to give international students an environment to speak English," said Sarah Galvin, coordinator of the Development Studies Program. "Instructors normally ask students to bring their own ideas to the class and exchange the ideas in English."

International students come from different cultural backgrounds and speak different native languages. They might be experienced in English grammar, sentence structure and vocabulary; however, conversational English is still a weak point for those who use English as an acquired language.

"As instructors in this program, we always encourage students to discuss their problems that they are facing in English. We try to make a pleasant atmosphere when running the program in class. This can encourage students to speak English. It can also help students to overcome difficulties in English," said Charles Coulston, a nuclear medicine technology professor who has volunteered to help with the ESL class.

According to Coulston, LCC President Dr. Jim Kerley strongly supports the faculty members' making connections with foreign cultures. Six LCC faculty members will make a visit to Changsha University in Hunan Province, China, to teach Chinese college students

▲ Charles Coulston, Nkongolo Kalala, and Stacy Webster-Little talk it over.

about American culture and English conversation. ESL at LCC is just one part of this cross-cultural program.

"I ... appreciate that LCC instructors have given us this great opportunity to speak English," said Bell Yakineko, a Japanese sophomore student in psychology major, who is taking the ESL program. "They have understood how international students struggle with a problem in learning English."

The ESL class introduces students to formal and informal English language skills, as well as the American culture, traditions, Americans' slang and customs. It can pilot you through the process of public speaking from the basic conversations to advanced comprehension and from mastering vocabularies to revising sentences. It is a special opportunity for international students to share their learning experiences with new friends from other parts of the earth.

To climb the ladder of success, everyone needs to eliminate obstacles and barriers. For every international student who has difficulty in English, just drop in any Thursday from 12:30-1:30 in MB 131 and sharpen your English skills.

Another focus area for faculty involved multicultural affairs and diversity training. LCC expanded its horizons in this area starting in 1995 when the Office of Multicultural Affairs was founded, according to the *LCC Courier*. In its October 2000 issue, the school newspaper interviewed Multicultural Affairs director Anthony Hartsfield, a Detroit native with a degree from Kentucky State University in Frankfort. Hartsfield pointed to a concentration by his office on minority recruiting, multicultural awareness, and diversity training. But there was more, he said: "I want students to know that this office in not just here for minority students." Hartsfield told the *LCC Courier* "the office is here to provide an inclusive environment that is respectful and inclusive to all students, so we can all benefit."

Multicultural Affairs Office gets the job done

BY FERRAN ROBINSON
CO-EDITOR

Since 1995 the Office of Multicultural Affairs at LCC has been promoting diversity enrichment at LCC. Anthony Hartsfield, a Kentucky State University graduate from Detroit, has been head of the office since February 1998. Hartsfield's office is focused on the areas of minority recruitment, multicultural awareness and diversity training for LCC and its students.

One of the primary functions of the office, multicultural recruitment, has been a strong aid in helping the school's enrollment to continue to grow. Hartsfield reports a 23% increase in African American students this year with 22% and 25% increases the past 2 years, respectively. Hartsfield says the school currently has about a 10% minority population.

"We're looking at probably close to almost 1000 African-American students alone," says Hartsfield.

Photo by Ferran Robinson
Anthony Hartsfield works to raise diversity awareness.

Since this interview the official African-American enrollment numbers came in at 733 students.

With a growing student minority population combined with a global post-college work environment, Hartsfield stresses the importance of diversity awareness. He says that the roles of colleges are changing to educate not just academically, but to educate socially with an emphasis on the appreciation for all cultures.

"I want students to know that this office is not just here for minority students," says Hartsfield "the office is here to provide an inclusive environment that is respectful and inclusive to all students, so we all can benefit."

To help serve and promote a diverse group of students, Hartsfield and the Multicultural Affairs Office are constantly working on events and training that have a culturally diverse emphasis. There are upcoming events relating to Hispanic Heritage Month in October, National Native American Heritage Month in November, and a Kwaanza celebration in December.

The biggest event in the works for the office is a "major international cultural day" which will take place in the spring. "The event will be a real big gala," says Hartsfield. He says it will be held outdoors and offer LCC students the chance to get acquainted with cultures from all over the world. People of different cultures from within the community and UK will be participating.

Hartsfield's efforts also include building on the duties of his office. "One area I'm continuing to build on is the area of diversity training for our faculty, staff and administrators here," says Hartsfield. He also says he would like to start a mentoring program on a pilot basis to help with the retention efforts of LCC students.

Hartsfield also says his goals also include getting more LCC involvement with Fayette County Public Schools and with the area's minority communities.

▼ Dr. Shirley Whitescarver, nursing professor, makes her point.

▼ Physics Professor Seetha Subramanian (left) confers with colleagues Joanne Olson-Biglieri and English Professor Carol Hunt.

▼ Librarian Marcia Freyman presents new information to eager faculty and staff, 1998.

▼ Faculty and staff enjoy Halloween.

▼ English Professor Don Boes also writes poetry.

▼ Mathematics Professor Vicki Partin (center) helps raise funds for Kentucky Educational Television (KET).

▼ Word Processing's
Tonya Spivey.

▼ Mathematics Professor
Larry Mullins.

▼ Communications Professor
Peggy Allen presides.

▼ Iva Boyatt's retirement party, where
she receives a well-earned crown.

▼ Nona Sparks
took care of
Word Processing
for a time.

Faculty & Staff

Lexington
Community College

Celebrate!

Radiology faculty member honored

A Lexington Community College faculty member has received one of the highest honors possible in her profession. Lucy LaFontaine, a radiography co-ordinator at LCC, has been awarded the Life Membership Award for Outstanding and Dedicated Service from the Kentucky Society of Radiologic Technologies.

LaFontaine

LaFontaine has taught at LCC since 1986 and has been a member of the radiology society for more than 30 years. Lexington Herald-Leader Wednesday, December 9, 1998

◀ Radiology Technology Professor Lucy LaFontaine was recognized for her service in the *Lexington Herald-Leader*, December 9, 1998.

▼ Professor Jan Hicks started her career as a nursing professor before teaching English. Here, Hicks receives some much-deserved recognition as the Carolyn Beam Award winner.

▲ Geography Professor Ryan Kelly won a Great Teacher Award.

▼ Professor Jim Matchuny wins a United Way prize.

▲ Members of the first class of Mandala Diversity Change Ambassadors. Kneeling, left to right: Diana Martin, Joe Anthony, and Kathy Dickison. Standing, left to right: Randolph Hollingsworth, Ben Worth, Carol Hunt, Shannon Bailey, and Erica Brownlee.

For the diversity-training element of the Multicultural Affairs program, LCC brought in former UK Vice Chancellor of Minority Affairs, Dr. William Parker, an impressive speaker and communicator with a missionary zeal for his task. Through his own business, Parker & Parker Associates, a diversity consulting firm, Parker teamed with the LCC Multicultural Affairs office and began the Mandala Movement Diversity Training Program. A mandala is an ancient representation of the universe from man's finite perspective, Hindu in origin, usually in the form of a circular object with multiple patterns and colors. Tibetan monks are world-renowned for their elaborate sand mandalas. According to online sources, "The Movement's mission is to create a cadre of people (faculty, staff, and community) who are culturally competent to create change" within LCC and Lexington. Mandala Movement Diversity Change Ambassadors, as program graduates were designated, would lead the way toward a more inclusive and tolerant environment, perhaps better to prepare students and others to the far-reaching and growing effects of globalization, and to "bring about a heightened sense of the value of cultural diversity, including a wide range of factors such as race, gender, age, economic status, life experiences, sexual orientation and disability."

LCC artist and professor Jacqui Linder used her sabbatical leave to create a beautiful multicolored mandala framed in wood. At first glance evocative of meticulous brush strokes, the mandala is not made of paint but rather tens of thousands of small pieces of paper cut from magazines, some 450,000, she estimated. "I cut the triangles the size of a housefly's wings from pictures of the physical world: flowers, bark, leaves, earth, water, rocks, sky, every kind of skin color and hair texture to give myself, as I created the mandala, a sense that I was creating something alive, integrated and inclusive," Linder said in the October 22, 2001, *UK News.* "When I got into collecting colors from magazine pictures, I found myself recreating this reddish-orange by gathering and mixing together every shade imaginable of red and orange along with browns and yellows, each individual triangle recognizable close up, but seen as solid red when viewed from afar." Linder saw the many colors as an expression of the cultural and ethnic diversity so apparent at Lexington Community College.

September 11, 2001

Celebrations of growth and diversity at LCC were perhaps never more important than on that sad day when the whole country and many more around the world watched the playing out of an entirely different world view with the barbarous destruction of the World Trade Center towers in New York City on September 11, 2001. Eyes were glued to television monitors in the Oswald Building lobby and elsewhere throughout the College, witnessing the death of thousands and the destruction and collapse of two massive symbols of American economic might in the heart of Manhattan. An attack on the Pentagon in Washington, D.C., and a failed attempt that ended on a field in Pennsylvania made it clear that this was a coordinated effort to kill Americans and destroy iconic institutions.

"Amid all the chaos," reported the *LCC Courier* of September 2001, "LCC students and faculty alike stood shocked, gather[ed] around televisions, watching the mayhem unfold. Emotions ran rampant, as many members of the LCC family were visibly shaken by what was happening just hours away.... 'I was in a total state of disbelief,'" said an English professor. "'At first, I thought it was just a devastating plane crash. I felt so bad for the victims, but it wasn't until later that I found out the sheer magnitude of the situation. After that, I was physically ill.'" One freshman reacted with both frustration and fear. Anthropology professor Leon Lane did not find the attack itself a surprise, even if he was surprised by its method and scale. "We do have to understand the roots and causes of the hatred directed toward us as a nation in order to fully understand and deal with the terrorist attacks," he said.

Dental hygiene student wins R. L. Bean Oral Radiology award. See page 7.

LCC students and faculty watch coverage of the Sept. 11 attacks, give their reactions. See page 3.

Georgetown College students donate blood at LCC. See page 10.

UK LEXINGTON COMMUNITY COLLEGE COURIER

Established 1998 Volume 5, Number 1   September 2001

Students roll up sleeves to help
Terrorist attacks inspire donors to give at blood drive

BY TIFFANY BOGGS, LAUREN
EVANS, ERIN O'BRIEN
STAFF WRITERS

When a tragedy occurs, individuals step up to the plate to lend a helping hand. This was evidenced by the blood drive held in the lobby of LCC's Academic-Technical Building on September 11 and 12, 2001.

Due to a sequence of unimaginable terrorists' destructions toward the World Trade Center and Pentagon, the need for blood donations suddenly became urgent on Sept. 11. In New York City and Washington, D.C., an enormous amount of injuries were sustained and lives were lost.

The Central Kentucky Blood Center was in full force under direction of Glen White, donor resources consultant. White, who had the LCC blood drive scheduled nine months in advance of the terrorist attacks, was overwhelmed with the high volume of individuals willing to donate

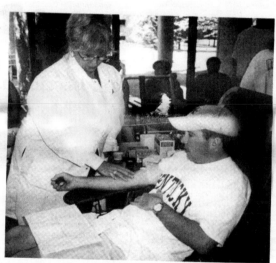
Photo by Kyle Keith
Matthew Winpelberg, a UK senior from Owensboro, said he waited in line to give blood from 10:30 a.m. until 2:30 p.m. Elizabeth Washburn, from Central Kentucky Blood Center, took Winpelberg's contribution.

blood, even those who normally wouldn't have.

Donors at the blood drive stated they felt helpless in the face of the tragedies and felt giving blood was their way of helping.

Some college students even traveled out of their district to help with the crisis. Angie Miracle, Andra Embry, Kristin Rosquist, and Staci Feazell traveled to LCC from Georgetown College. The Georgetown College students were directed to LCC from the Central Kentucky Blood Center, which was overrun with citizens wanting to donate blood.

Out of the four, Angie Miracle was the only student who was originally planning to donate. However, after her friends heard about the plea for blood in New York and Washington, D.C., they decided to also pull up their sleeves and help save lives.

See BLOOD, page 10

LCC community stunned by events of Sept. 11

BY JOE SCULLY
STAFF WRITER

September 11, 2001 will forever be remembered as one of the darkest days in this nation's history.

At approximately 8:45 a.m., American Airlines Flight 11 crashed into the north tower of the World Trade Center in New York City. Just 18 minutes later, a stunned nation watched in horror as a second plane, United Airlines Flight 175 crashed into the World Trade Center's south tower. At 9:40 a.m., a mere 37 minutes after the

second plane crash, American Airlines Flight 77 was crashed into the U.S. Pentagon in Washington, D.C. Twenty minutes after the Pentagon attack, another airliner, United Airlines Flight 93 crashed in Pennsylvania, about 80 miles southeast of Pittsburgh.

Amid all the chaos, LCC students and faculty alike stood shocked, gather around televisions, watching the mayhem unfold. Emotions ran rampant, as many members of the LCC family were visibly shaken by what was happening just hours away.

Many of the students and faculty

could simply not believe what they were witnessing.

"I was in a total state of disbelief," said Lori Guiseppi, an English professor at LCC. "At first, I thought it was just a devastating plane crash. I felt so bad for the victims, but it wasn't until later that I found out the sheer magnitude of the situation. After that, I was physically ill."

Jessica Bush, an LCC freshman, had another perspective. "My first reaction was frustration. It was totally uncalled for, and I was also very scared."

Others, such as anthropology

instructor Leon Lane, were not so surprised. "I was not shocked," said Lane. "No one who studies world affairs would be. I was surprised by the scale of the attack and the method in which it was carried out, but not by the fact that we were a target of terrorism.

"We do have to understand the roots and causes of the hatred directed toward us as a nation," Lane continued, "in order to fully understand and deal with the terrorist attacks."

Lane stressed that the United States must seek justice, rather than retribution.

See ATTACKS, page 7

▲ The 2000 SACS Accreditation Steering Committee. Seated, left to right: Erla Mowbray, Sandy Carey, Joanne Olson-Biglieri, and Art Dameron. Standing, left to right: Becky Womack, Jake Gibbs, Eileen Abel, Debbie Holt, Janella Spencer, Cindy Barber, and Peggy Saunier.

One important measure of the academic viability of a school and its programs is provided by means of accreditation. In a society as obsessed with credentials as the United States, no college-level program could hope for success without the proper acknowledgement of its region's accreditation organization. For Kentucky, that meant approval from the Southern Association of Colleges and Schools (SACS). Every ten years, the College found itself subjected to an intense, across-the-board scrutiny from top to bottom. Most educators would agree that it is a healthy process, with involvement required by administrators, faculty, and staff. Accreditation strengthens academic programs through its self-study process, as it identifies where programmatic strengths and weaknesses lie. Areas in need of correction are marked and areas deserving of imitation heralded. After all the information is gathered and processed, a detailed report is prepared. A SACS Reaffirmation Committee visits the school to inspect programs, processes, and results before it renders its final judgment.

Year 2000's SACS reaffirmation process proved more of a challenge than previously expected. The process itself began in 1998, with appointment of a twelve-member committee. Literally everyone in the College was involved in the process to one degree or another. *Everyone.* In the final analysis, programs proved sound, courses offered were deemed appropriate, and standards held were judged suitable for a community college. The

SACS commission did "not question LCC's overall academic quality." But one observer of the SACS process told the *Lexington Herald-Leader* on July 9, 2002, that "If an institution has separate accreditation, we just want to be sure it has control over its own destiny." LCC's accreditation had been extended, but until the autonomy issue was addressed satisfactorily, the school was on probation. In a July 3, 2003 letter, SACS posited that LCC "has not yet demonstrated that it has sufficient autonomy to be accredited separately" from the University of Kentucky. LCC had held separate SACS accreditation from UK since it opened in 1965. But the SACS accreditation emphasis had changed. SACS had "begun to consider more carefully whether institutions such as community colleges should receive independent accreditation if, for all intents and purposes, they are part of a larger institution."

An accreditation consultant was scheduled to revisit LCC in late July 2003. The College was eligible for an additional year of probation, but after that LCC must meet the SACS definition of autonomy or face losing separate accreditation. UK provost and chief academic officer Mike Nietzel indicated to the *Herald-Leader* that the University had made "changes it thought were sufficient" for LCC's reaccreditation. But "LCC is part of UK," said Nietzel, "and we want it to remain part of the University of Kentucky." If separate accreditation became impossible, LCC could be accredited through UK, said Nietzel.

In a July 28, 2003, *Lexington Herald-Leader* editorial, President Kerley felt compelled to clarify LCC's position. It was all about autonomy, he said, not quality of the institution and its programs. "About 80 percent of the work has been accomplished to satisfy SACS," wrote Kerley, "such as approving our technical programs separately from the university, and gaining independence to raise funds for the institution." Graduate alumni of LCC surveyed reported satisfaction with their educational experience at the College. Students at LCC liked the UK connection. Large numbers of LCC students transferred to UK, Eastern Kentucky University, and elsewhere. "In fact," Kerley noted, "more students have transferred from LCC than from all the other community colleges combined." To Kerley, the bottom line was that "LCC is a dynamic institution that provides opportunities for many people to achieve their dreams."

That essentially left UK and LCC three possible avenues to address autonomy and separate accreditation. As reported in the December 10, 2003, *Lexington Herald-Leader*, under one scenario LCC could become more independent but remain part of UK. This was the solution favored by most LCC faculty. Or LCC could remain with UK but lose separate accreditation. LCC would be accredited under UK's own institutional accreditation with SACS. But President Kerley opined that this was "not an option" because it would not allow LCC to continue its open access policy under UK's selective admissions policy. "Our admissions policy could change and we could simply become a remedial college for a big research university," said Kerley. "I'm not sure we would be a priority." UK Provost Nietzel admitted in an interview that the problem now appeared larger than it had beforehand. He relayed that a consultant on the project stated, "You guys are just rearranging the deck chairs and it's not even close" to answering the SACS recommendation. The dilemma especially for technical program faculty was encapsulated by LCC dental lab technology professor Robin Gornto: "I would prefer to stay with UK, but we have to keep our separate accreditation."

Option three would have allowed LCC to maintain its separate accreditation, but it would have to sever its UK governance and join the Kentucky Community and

> *It was all about autonomy, [President Kerley] said, not quality of the institution and its programs.*

Technical College System, KCTCS, that governed the other thirteen community colleges once under the UK aegis. In his assessment of this option, Kerley agreed that "there could be real financial advantages" for LCC if it joined KCTCS, because the College to that point received "much less funding and building space per pupil than other community colleges" in Kentucky. Students at LCC generally did not like this idea, however. "I don't know if I'd want to go here" if LCC was no longer part of UK, one freshman was quoted as saying. Another freshman told the *Herald-Leader* that she was concerned about credits earned and their transferability. Credits would transfer to UK or elsewhere just as they did from other community colleges. But "I think people like feeling like they're part of UK," this student said. Many more could be found with the same viewpoint. Indeed, about 80 percent of students, faculty, and staff at LCC wanted to remain with UK, according to a report in the February 10, 2004, *Herald-Leader*. As for the possibility of merger with KCTCS, system president Michael McCall responded with a politically acceptable answer: "We support the university in whatever it decides. If they decide to transfer to us, we will be more than happy to work with them." Otherwise, it was too early for commentary on any details such a merger might entail, said McCall.

▲ Petition drive to keep LCC with UK.

Finally the autonomy issue played against LCC remaining with UK. Even in December 2003, UK president Dr. Lee Todd was unclear whether he would accede to a change in UK's nearly forty-year connection with LCC. Jim Kerley reiterated "It's very, very important for us to keep close ties with the university," reported the *Lexington Herald-Leader* on December 10, 2003. As for Dr. Todd, he indicated that he was "not ready yet. It's a significant decision" to determine whether or not to change the relationship between UK and LCC.

Some former UK officials saw something more afoot than the public banter indicated. Dr. Wethington, who as UK president had opposed the original separation of the other thirteen community colleges from the University's governance, and who similarly opposed LCC's separation, thought that the decision already had been made before the final stamp of approval came down to the UK Board of Trustees meeting in February 2004. It seemed that the UK administration was not going to do anything other than let the debate play out. While UK continued to affirm that it wanted to keep LCC with the University, officials also contended

> **The tide of change seemed to be sweeping LCC out away from its UK moorings.**

that they wanted what was "best" for LCC, and intimated that that might mean transfer of governance to KCTCS.

The tide of change seemed to be sweeping LCC out away from its UK moorings. The UK Board of Trustees academic affairs committee recommended the change. From there, it went to the UK Board of Trustees, the *prima facie* final voice on the matter of governance. The UK Board cited money as a chief consideration in reaching its decision. LCC received $1,294 per student, while KCTCS received $4,223, according to the February 10, 2004, *Herald-Leader*. One Board member pointed to this discrepancy in support of LCC joining KCTCS. Otherwise, she said, "we deny students the opportunity they deserve."

Of course, the issue did not involve only a new administrative arrangement; it also threatened a new physical location for the College. Just where that location might be remained highly problematic. The Cooper Campus buildings proved especially controversial. No secret could hide the fact that UK wanted more space, and the Cooper Campus would address such space concerns nicely. On the other hand, LCC claimed some

Alumni Association offers benefits to LCC grads

BY COURTNEY HAMMONS
STAFF REPORTER

As graduation draws near for the class of 2002, these students will become LCC alumni with a free-one year membership to the Lexington Community College Alumni Association whether they decide to be active in the organization or not.

Although it does not fit all criteria of an official association, this affiliate club has named itself an association since at least 1992. Becoming a member in the LCC Alumni Association includes an invitation for membership in the University of Kentucky Alumni Association as well. Membership to the association is available to graduates and alumni.

Members, ranging in numbers from 300 to 350, must pay $10 each year while graduates automatically join for free their first year. The yearly dues go into a fund that later go directly back to each member through

parties, refreshments, and door prizes. Other money raised or donated by members goes toward the scholarship fund.

Julie Weidmer, Director of Alumni Affairs, said the goal of the association is "to build more relationships." Weidmer describes this organization as "friend raising instead of fund raising."

Although graduates will always be LCC alumni, there are many benefits of becoming and staying an active member of the association. Members receive access to lower arena basketball tickets, check out privileges at the library, and two annual copies of the Alumni News, the official newsletter of this association. Members can participate in the annual LCC Homecoming Tailgate Party and the annual Graduation Pizza Party.

To learn more about the LCC and UK Alumni Associations contact Julie Wiedmer via e-mail at jwwied0@uky.edu or call 257-3723.

◀ Dr. Jim Kerley wears his academic regalia well.

BENEFITS OF ALUMNI ASSOCIATION MEMBERSHIP

* the first year is free
* opportunity to purchase lower-arena basketball tickets
* participation in the annual graduation pizza party
* participation in the homecoming tailgate party
* check-out privileges at the library
* receive alumni newsletter

Incoming UK president eyes top-20 status

Dr. Lee Todd selected to succeed Wethington

BY MELISSA LIPPERT
STAFF WRITER

Todd

The UK board of trustees voted unanimously on January 23 to choose Dr. Lee T. Todd Jr. as the school's eleventh president.

Todd, a Kentucky native and 1968 UK graduate, will begin his term on July 1. Todd will be at the helm to lead faculty, staff and 31,000 students into the twenty-first century.

After reviewing feedback from UK students and citizens all across Kentucky, the board of trustees decided Todd was committed to the University of Kentucky and to the state of Kentucky as well.

"I want to find out what makes a top-20 school, have the money to create it, oversee a $600 million dollar capital campaign, and connect with the faculty, staff, and students," Todd said in a recent interview with the *Herald-Leader.*

The selection committee underwent a nine-month process in which to choose candidates and named three finalists on January 10.

According to information on the UK web site, one finalist chose to become provost of Iowa State University, while the other candidate decided the time for him was not right, withdrawing his name from consideration only minutes before the board chose Todd.

Todd, an executive vice-president for Lotus Development Company for the last 17 years, has sta' in recent interviews that he is con' a he will be able to raise the per c a income and succeed with the co. ge's land-grant mission.

" I am glad the University of Kentucky was able to select a representative that is a Kentucky native, as well as one who will help the school reach top-20 recognition," said Jesica Poland, a junior economics and management major.

---

ownership of the buildings and pointed to College fund-raising that had gone to improvement of the physical plant. The UK Board considered a resolution that gave LCC a "minimum" of five years to stay on Cooper Campus and charged UK to be "responsible for helping the community college find a new, much larger home as enrollment grows." Kerley asserted that such a proposal was totally "unacceptable."

Lee Todd "made it clear that he thinks the move could help both schools move forward: LCC to become a bigger and better community college, and UK to become a top 20 research university." Todd told LCC's assembled faculty and staff that "I think you'd be the gem of that system—you'd have a better chance for funding, and your mission is commensurate with KCTCS," the February 10, 2004, *Lexington Herald-Leader* reported.

In an unusual, even emotion-charged meeting, the question of LCC's relationship with the University was answered. UK's Board of Trustees transferred LCC governance away from the University after thirty-nine years. Only one additional layer of approval remained, the Kentucky General Assembly, and a cadre of LCC students, faculty, and staff vowed to take the fight to the legislature. But that avenue ultimately turned out to be nothing more than a mere detour from the inevitable. LCC Student Government president

Margaret Morgan met with Kentucky Governor Ernie Fletcher in Frankfort and came away from the meeting convinced the governor was on LCC's side. But a spokesman for the governor said that Fletcher supported the UK Board's decision, as reported in the February 10, 2004, *Herald-Leader.* On the other hand, the governor's spokesman did indicate that Fletcher believed that certain ties between the two schools should be maintained: "[I]t is a logical, reasonable decision only if the historical and cultural association with the University of Kentucky is preserved."

Not even the UK Board was unanimous in the vote to separate LCC from UK governance. Paducah's representative left the meeting in a huff after stating "You've been fed a bunch of faddle, some of it true, most of it untrue" about the need for and nature of separation. Dr. Todd continued to forward the notion of separation: "I think the best case is for these two institutions to focus on the two different missions we have," he told reporters. In a February 12, 2004, editorial in the *Lexington Herald-Leader,* Dr. Kerley wrote that the autonomy issue "could have had a successful resolution, and LCC could have remained with UK. But that clearly was not Todd's wish; he preferred to separate LCC from UK." LCC Spanish professor Ninfa Floyd voiced the notion that many adopted following the UK Board vote: "It's done, it's over; we have to accept it and move on."

KENTUCKY VOICES

May Cuba be free by Castro's next birthday

By Ninfa Floyd

Flashback to Dec. 31, 1958: a wide-eyed, pixyish, 10-year-old strolls through the crowded, cobblestone streets of her native city, Santa Clara, Cuba.

All around her, hoards of smiling, jubilant, townspeople seem to have the same purpose: to laugh, to hug one another and to shake the hand of a ragtag army of bearded, smiling men in their olive-drab uniforms and with rosaries hanging from their necks.

Ninfa Floyd is a professor of Spanish at Bluegrass Community and Technical College (formerly Lexington Community College).

That night, a family celebration, a toast to the New Year: To Che, Camilo and Fidel; to the liberation of Cuba from Fulgencio Batista, to his cowardly departure from the island and to a wide open future filled with hope, and dreams of justice.

See TOAST, D4

Spanish Professor Ninfa Floyd contributed editorial works to the *Lexington Herald-Leader.*

TOAST | May Cubans not have to celebrate Castro's next birthday

From Page D1

Flash forward to Aug. 13, 2005: The leader of that ragtag army celebrates his 79th birthday as the longest-serving, non-elected political leader of any nation in the world

That girl, now a woman and not so pixyish any more, with eyes that have seen the passing years erode and cancel out the hopes and dreams of her generation, makes another toast: To the Cuban people, may you soon feel the breeze of freedom and justice blow over your island.

And to Fidel. In the 79th August of your life may you feel real remorse, sadness, guilt and deep regret for:

Fidel Castro, who turned 79 on Aug. 13, has ruled Cuba for more than 45 years.

■ All the Cuban lives lost fighting your imperial adventures in Angola and Latin America in pursuit of your megalomaniacal obsession to become the Simon Bolivar of the 20th century.

■ All the Cubans who have died before your firing squads, in your prisons and from beatings, starvation and overwork.

■ The 2003 firing squad deaths of three Cubans whose only crime was to hijack a boat to escape an island that has become a virtual prison for its people.

■ The deaths of the men, women and children who have thrown themselves into the ocean's stormy waters aboard primitive rafts made of wooden planks and the black inner tubes of tires in the hope of reaching Florida.

■ The past year's arrests and summary sentencing of 75 peaceful dissidents, writers, journalists and human-rights activists to 10 to 25 years in prison for the crime of backing the Varela Project, a petition drive seeking political, civil and economic freedoms in Cuba's constitution.

■ The economic devastation of Cuba, which continues to sink in a record high foreign debt caused by your outdated Cuban model: a dictator at the top, surrounded by military men who hold political power, control repressive forces and direct and manage the major enterprises of production.

■ Your financial gains and riches, your life of splendor and Forbes magazine's "honorable" mention of you in its list of the top 50 richest men in the world.

■ The spiritual sadness and moral devastation of my people, who live suspended from a thread, always wondering whether the next day will bring more electrical shortages, food shortages and revolutionary slogans, ideology and demands.

■ Your irreversible, fanatical self-delusions that humankind is on your side.

■ Your mind-boggling indifference to the plight of your people.

And may this be the last August of your life.

In spite of all the rhetoric that surrounded the accreditation issue, that, too, could have been avoided, according to Wethington. Wethington confessed to feeling "hurt" that LCC's accreditation was threatened in the first place. "I thought that was most unfortunate. In my opinion, these accreditation issues were not insurmountable and could have been resolved to the satisfaction of SACS if the University had chosen to meet SACS requirements. This was a University of Kentucky decision, and rightly so because LTI/LCC was established by the UK Board of Trustees. As it turned out, by the time the UK Board of Trustees was meeting to 'decide' the fate of the UK-LCC connection, I believe the decision had already been made by the UK administration. Convincing the Board or, even later, the state legislature not to proceed with separation was not an issue. The Board and legislature were not pushing separation. Evidently the UK administration advocated separation to the UK Board which made the decision to cut LCC's formal ties to UK."

Jim Kerley saw Lexington Community College as a "great access point" for many who wished to pursue a course of study in college. "We gave so many individuals an opportunity to further their education in a non-elitist way," he wrote. Further, LCC's reputation as a transfer community college, with solid pre-baccalaureate programs that prepared students well for their final two years in pursuit of a bachelor's degree, was "excellent." In the minds of the College faculty, none of this would change.

Kerley's regret was the change in governance. "I think UK missed a golden opportunity with the LCC connection; we could have made this a national model," he wrote, a "community college working with a research university." But while strong relations with the University undoubtedly would continue, it would not be the same.

While many LCC advocates were dismayed with the separation, not all felt the change to be a negative one. Paul Taylor, for twenty-eight years an administrator with LTI/LCC, saw the change to join with the Kentucky Community and Technical College System as "a great thing." President Todd gave up much when

he cut loose LCC, said Taylor. Todd and UK "gave up the farm to let LCC go," he said in an interview. "UK could have kept us but didn't want to," he continued, primarily because of the focus on UK obtaining top-twenty status among public research universities. Added Taylor, "Had Wethington been at UK, this never would have happened."

One question that bothered many faculty and students as well was whether the reconstituted LCC would be able to retain its buildings on the Cooper Campus. "I think a lot of that will depend upon the UK administration over time," observed Wethington. "There will be continued interest on the part of the University faculty and administration in having LCC be located somewhere else. Nothing will happen in the short term," he predicted, "because of the action of the General Assembly. There is an assumption that LCC can stay where it is as long as it wants to stay." But, stated Wethington, "What will likely happen over time is that LCC will get big enough and the community college operation itself, KCTCS, will start looking at ways to get that institution located somewhere else. And if and when that happens the University will likely be much interested and willing to cooperate in moving it somewhere else. But I don't see anything happening in the short term because I think the legislators are not going to let something happen unless LCC and KCTCS want it to happen."

Dr. Wethington in an interview made another rather important observation regarding the future of the College. "I think LCC will be fine. It will do well. The combination with the technical school will benefit students. The commitment to support the College is still there, and it will do well. I think it would have done well had it remained a part of UK, and I think both it and UK would have been well served by having this operation continue to be a part of the University of Kentucky. I think the University of Kentucky will be the one that will suffer most from this separation." In another interview, former UK Medical Center Chancellor Peter P. Bosomworth proposed a more cautious prophecy: that it would take about ten years to evaluate whether or not the separation actually was a good thing for either UK or LCC.

> *The commitment to support the College is still there, and it will do well.*

But on June 30, 2004, an agreement between UK and KCTCS regarding LCC's transfer to the latter organization was signed. It would be a gradual move. LCC students could still buy UK basketball and football tickets, live in UK dormitories, use UK libraries, access UK gymnasiums and other athletic facilities, and even continue participation in UK intramural events. LCC's Cooper Campus buildings remained UK property, but LCC could stay rent-free for "as long as necessary." Faculty and staff were given a "choice," either to remain in UK's pay and benefit system or switch to KCTCS. Many faculty and staff did not like the change; others were pleased to be "done" with the autonomy and accreditation issues.

Programmatically, nothing changed. For a time, the name Lexington Community College continued as the official designation of the College. In 2005, the consolidation process with Central Kentucky Technical College began, resulting in a name change for the newly merged institution. Bluegrass Community and Technical District was used until December 2005, when SACS formally approved the consolidation; afterward, the new College name was Bluegrass Community and Technical College (BCTC). Bluegrass offered technical programs just as had Lexington Community College, and the standards for those programs remained the same. Pre-baccalaureate faculty would require the same standard of performance in class as before, the better to prepare students for transfer to a four-year program. Clearly, most of the change came in administration, in bureaucracy, and in nomenclature.

Most students initially seemed unhappy with the decision. Others adapted quickly, while some did not care. But many students had held dear the connection with the University of Kentucky. "I think UK is losing out on a wonderful institution," an LCC sophomore told the July 1, 2004, *Lexington Herald-Leader.* "I think they're hurting themselves in the long run." It was an opinion often heard during those days. Time alone would tell whether that assessment held true. Whatever the later evaluation might be, it was time now for everyone to move forward.

The Academic Technical Building on Cooper Drive on a beautiful spring day.

Lexington Community College experienced thirty-nine years of successful operation and growth under the governance of the University of Kentucky. It was a relationship that was mutually beneficial. To look back upon the history of the UK-LCC/LTI association during those years, it is clear that Lexington Technical Institute first and then Lexington Community College fulfilled the mission set before it. Quality technical programs were coupled with solid preparation for a bachelor's degree program through transfer; all found a home at Lexington Community College. Thousands of students benefited from the opportunities presented by the Institute and the College, and moved on to have careers and lives better than might otherwise have been possible.

Numbers tell part of the story. From 1965, when LTI opened, twenty students total entered the two technical programs offered, dental laboratory technology and nursing. In 2004, the student headcount was 8,808, and LCC offered over a dozen technical programs and many other avenues of study. In 1968–69, LTI had actual operating expenditures of $134,266; academic year 2003–04 saw expenses measured at $28,216,311. By 2004, LCC had twenty-six full-time faculty members with doctorates of various stripes, most faculty members with master's degrees, some with more than one master's degree, and many similarly credentialed part-time faculty.

These are positive statistics from an institutional standpoint. But there are other measures that might be consulted. For example, LTI and LCC worked closely with numerous community partners. In the earliest years of LTI development, probably the two most

◄ Sociology Professor David Wachtel (left) accompanies President Kerley and a delegation of Chinese educators from the Young Library on UK's main campus.

important associations with the Institute's programs were the University of Kentucky Medical Center and Lexington's International Business Machines (IBM) facility. Years later, the UK Medical Center connection remained vital to certain health-related programs. Many other businesses, industries, banks, and institutions had associated themselves closely with LTI and LCC. Toyota has worked with the College, and so too has the Lexington Bluegrass Chamber of Commerce. Advisory boards made up of prominent members of the private sector helped advise and guide many LCC programs. Many UK faculty, staff, and administration worked closely with LCC counterparts, and worked with them well.

To Marie Piekarski, the most striking aspect of Lexington Technical Institute and Lexington Community College was the teaching and training, with the resultant graduates. "The most outstanding success of LTI and the Community College System," she told an interviewer, "is producing thousands of health care workers throughout the state." Perhaps at first there was some peering down of noses toward the community colleges by University faculty and administrators, stated Piekarski, but "We made many converts over the years among University faculty." And Piekarski gave the credit to such success to the many faculty members of the College: "One has to marvel at the preparation of our faculty in community colleges," she said.

Another source of insight comes from the thoughts and reflections of a few of the many people connected

▲ Left to right: Stony Smith, Sunil Yajnik, Veronica Miller, Julie McClanahan, and Mary Ann Whipple.

with the LTI and LCC operation, a smattering of those many who felt the influence of the Institute or the College on their lives. For example, when Tri Roberts was a student at UK studying psychology from 1968 to 1973, he could not recall ever having heard of LTI. Then a friend's father working in respiratory therapy got him interested in learning the trade, and Roberts was off on a new career, one that would lead him from practitioner to teacher to administrator with LTI and then with LCC. Pat McDermott similarly rose from the ranks, starting as a member of the first class of dental laboratory technology students, then working as an academic practitioner and teacher, then back to private practice. Both have expressed their satisfaction with their LTI student experience.

Dr. Helen Reed passes at 92, leaves behind gift of inspiration

Educator shared story with colleague 3 months before death

BY JAMES B. GOODE
PROFESSOR

If one travels down the hallway of the Moloney Building on the campus of Lexington Community College and stops by the Writing Center in Room 150, on most days he will find a neatly dressed, tall, regal woman with beautiful, white hair and a tanned face. If one pays close attention, he will discover that she has an infectious smile and a voice filled with gentle assurance. She patiently tutors students of all ages who are enrolled in writing classes—from those who are just out of high school to those returning to school after having been in the work world for years. Sometimes one will find her sitting in the student commons area chatting with a table full of students barely a tenth her age.

Almost no one would suspect that she is 92. No one would suspect that she has been teaching for 64 years. No one would

suspect that she holds a B.A. in English, a M.A. in Psychology & Guidance, and a Ph.D. in Higher Education Administration. No one would suspect that she has taught in one-room schools, graded schools, high schools—that she has been a high school principal, a college professor, and a military commander.

Reed's story is an American story. Her story chronicles what it means to emerge from humble means and move to the head of the class. Her story is one of strength, endurance, and focus. Her story is about just one of heroes who stayed stateside and formed a vast infrastructure which supported the soldiers returning from the war in the Pacific and European theaters. This is a story of giving—of being concerned for the welfare of others. This is a story of a woman who has lived her life by a simple code handed down from her mother: "One should never mistreat a stranger because they might be an

angel!"

This story begins 165 miles north of Kansas City at Pleasanton, Iowa in 1910 and with a family of tenant farmers who struggled to eke out a living by raising corn and wheat on a 680-acre farm with little or no machinery. It begins in a place where, in the summer, it was so hot they had to work the fields at midnight to stand the oppressive heat.

Helen Reed, the eldest of 13 children, survived the flu epidemic of 1918. She survived the trauma of having her baby sister die in her arms when she was only eight years

See REED, Page 4

Photo by James Goode

◀ LCC S.W.A.T. team.

▼ Some LCC students lounge with the Kentucky Thoroughblades hockey team mascot.

Give Duke the decade, Cats claim the century

By: Tony Radden

There's been a lot of talk lately among college basketball fans about the team of the 1990s. Waste of time. As far as this semi-rational Kentucky fan is concerned, let Duke have their measly decade. The new millennium is upon us; it's time to set the record straight about the undisputed team of the century-Kentucky.

Actually, at this point, undisputed is not accurate, for many "experts" as well as armchair point guards will dispute that UCLA's dominance under John Wooden solidifies the Bruins claim to T.O.C. Before I am accused of being biased (which I am, but that's not important), let me just say that although I wasn't born until 1977, I've seen, read, and heard plenty about the UCLA dynasty of the 60s and 70s. Amazing. Ten national championships in twelve years, including seven in a row. What they did will never come close to being duplicated. 'Nuff props and credit and respect to John Wooden and the UCLA Bruins for what they accomplished in the 1960s and 1970s.

With that being said, let me also say this: I am no mathematician. Hell, I'm a 22-year-old freshman At Lexington Community College. So by all means, please correct me if I'm wrong, but the last time I checked, a century consisted of a whole lot more than just two decades.

Ask yourself this; What has UCLA done since John Wooden retired ? And for that matter ,what did they do before he showed up? Since his retirement in 1975, UCLA has won one national championship; Kentucky's won three. Before Westwood had their wizard, the Bruins won a whopping zero national titles to UK's four. Isn't there something to be said for longevity? Consistency? Two in the forties, two in the fifties, two in the nineties, one in the seventies and six other final four appearances throughout the century for the Wildcats.

UCLA is number one in national championships, Kentucky is number two. Kentucky is number one in all-time victories, UCLA is not even in the top four! So the University of Kentucky's men's basketball program is in the top two in both national championships and all-time victories. No one else can say that. Are you convinced yet?

In 1948, UK coach Adolph Rupp coached the United States Olympic basketball team. The nucleus of that team was made up of Kentucky's back-to-back national championship teams. They won a gold medal. Can you imagine if Mike Kryzewski or Bill Gutheridge took their college team and won an Olympic gold medal today? The media would proclaim them great American heroes and their school (Duke or North Carolina) would be dubbed instantly the one with the richest tradition. Too bad the media circus that exists today didn't back then (actually maybe that's a good thing).

Some schools have basketball teams. Few schools have basketball programs. Only four of those traditions rich enough to be considered a program have won national championships under two different coaches. UCLA, North Carolina, Indiana, and Kansas. Cute. Kentucky has won national championships under four, count them, four different coaches-Adolph Rupp, Joe B. Hall, Rick Pitino, and Tubby Smith, proving that it's not just the coach, but the program itself that is strong.

Don't get me wrong here, we're not a perfect program (as a native Kentuckian, I'm allowed to say "we"). We've broken the rules before, and we've paid the price. But, we've always resurfaced to our rightful place on top. It took us going on probation for Carolina to surpass us in all-time wins. They have been spectacular ever since, but we've been better, leapfrogging them back to number one all-time less than a decade after being punished (rightfully) by the NCAA. True, the Tar Heels have a decisive lead in the head-to-head series with UK, but that's about as much as they can claim towards their T.O.C. argument (three national titles, how nice).

Please disregard my environment for the sake of this argument. If I were from Los Angeles, Chapel Hill, Bloomington or Lawrence I would still think that Kentucky was the team of the century (although I probably wouldn't admit it). It's like when you're mom tells you that you're the handsomest boy in the world, when she knows good and well that I'm the handsomest boy in the world. She tries to convince herself that what she has is the best because it's hers. So I will admit, there are several other college basketball programs that are very handsome indeed, but they all appear quite homely when standing next to seven national championships, more wins than any other school, more tournament appearances than any other school, more finishes in the top ten than any other school, more conference championships than every other school in the SEC combined (say what you will, but it is a power conference), an Olympic gold medal and four different coaches wearing rings. We are the team of the century, we are Kentucky. I'm Tony Radden, good night. (Applause)

▼ He loves science:
Dr. Norm Strobel.

▼ Environmental Science Technology
Professor Jean Watts (right).

▼ Physics Professor
Bill Luyster.

▼ Always a friendly face
in Karen Mayo.

▼ Architectural Technology
Professor Bill Batson.

▼ Professor Brent Eldridge concocts some curious potion.

▼ English Professors Joe Anthony, Sandy Carey, and Ben Worth seem to enjoy tea and crumpets.

▼ English Professor Lori Houghton.

▼ Geography Professor Valiant Norman.

Faculty & Staff

Lexington
Community College

Another former student, Doug King, remarked that to him, "Lexington Community College represented 'what was attainable.' Hopes and dreams came to light; career goals and prospects were within reach and furthering my education had become a viable option. Lexington Community College carried course work that was relevant to the times as well as practical in application. My professors and teachers challenged me to exceed my own expectations. In doing so, I was able to complete a double major in less than three years. I consider their friendship and camaraderie as valuable as the courses themselves. The teachers were approachable outside of the academic realm and quick to engage in conversation or assistance when needed. A college education can be looked upon as an investment in one's future. At LCC, I would have to say, it was time well spent."

A student from Louisville, Michael Riggs, who went on to earn a bachelor's degree from the University of Kentucky, assessed his LCC education this way: "Though people often perceive the community college system to be inferior to larger universities, I did not find this to be the case at Lexington Community College. Lexington Community College provided me with the necessary skills to further my education at the University of Kentucky. The faculty at Lexington Community College during my years there held themselves to the same high educational standards as I found in the faculty at the University of Kentucky. Throughout the years, Lexington Community College has proven to be a valuable stepping stone for many students in their pursuit of higher education."

Many more student testimonials might be found. Jonni Parks began her association with LCC because of the UK tie, she recalled. Full-time work and school challenged Parks, but she noted that she "was able to get instruction from great professors" at LCC. Nathan Schuler enjoyed his program of study in Organizational Management in a two-plus-two arrangement between LCC and Midway College. Boyle County student Cathy Black summed up her thoughts by writing she just "loved" Lexington Community College.

Many more similarly styled comments could be found. Some negative comments could be found, too. No place is perfect. But the many people who have worked and studied at Lexington Technical Institute and Lexington Community College over the years have every right to be proud of that association, and of the many contributions made to the greater Lexington

Artist's conception of a proposed new Cooper campus building.

◀ Architectural Technology Professor Tom Rogers (center).

▲ Students come from many different backgrounds, with different measures of experience. Here, Mary Hahn (right) and Harriet Anderson from The Lafayette at Country Place retirement community in Lexington have some fun on LCC computers.

community and to the University of Kentucky. Many UK alumni can trace their start to LTI, or LCC, or one of the other community colleges formerly in the UK Community College System. Many would say that the community college was a good place for them to start their college experiences. In that, they would be in good company. According to the American Council on Education study *College Students Today: A National Portrait* (November 2005), of the 87 percent of all postsecondary students in the United States who are undergraduates, 40 percent attend community colleges.

Lexington Community College and Lexington Technical Institute had a long and successful run as part of the University of Kentucky. Many strong ties remained after the change in governance. A new chapter opened in the life of the College once it joined the Kentucky Community and Technical College System. But aside from the administrative change, the faculty members and the courses they taught remained the same. The technical programs still meet the demands of their fields of study; the pre-baccalaureate courses of study remain as before; the standards did not diminish. There was every good reason to believe that the College would continue its good work for its students and the community. Lexington, central Kentucky, and all the students yet to come deserve nothing less.

Students and staff congregate by the school sign
next to the Moloney Building on Cooper Drive.

Tables

Appendix

Directors and Presidents of Lexington Technical Institute and Lexington Community College, 1965–2005

Term	Name	Position
University of Kentucky Lexington Technical Institute		
1965–66	Edsel T. Godbey	Director
1966–67	Charles T. Wethington	Director
1967–70	G. Robert Boyd	Director
1970–73	M. L. Archer	Director
1974–84	William N. Price	Director
University of Kentucky Lexington Community College		
1984–85	Sharon B. Jaggard	Acting Director
1985–86	Sharon B. Jaggard	Director
1986	Ben W. Carr	Acting Director
1986–93	Allen G. Edwards	Director and President
1993–94	Tony Newberry	Acting President
1994–97	Janice N. Friedel	President
1997–98	James P. Chapman	Acting President
1998–2007*	A. James Kerley	President

* Dr. Kerley oversaw the transition of Lexington Community College from its governance under the University of Kentucky to the Kentucky Community and Technical College System as the Bluegrass Community and Technical College, beginning in 2005. Dr. Kerley resigned in 2007 to take the presidency of Gulf Coast Community College in Florida.

Governors of Kentucky 1959–2005

Governor	Party	Term
Bert T. Combs	Democrat	1959–63
Edward "Ned" Breathitt	Democrat	1963–67
Louie B. Nunn	Republican	1967–71
Wendell Ford	Democrat	1971–74
Julian Carroll	Democrat	1974–79
John Y. Brown, Jr.	Democrat	1979–83
Martha Layne Collins	Democrat	1983–87
Wallace Wilkinson	Democrat	1987–91
Brereton C. Jones	Democrat	1991–95
Paul E. Patton	Democrat	1995–2003*
Ernie Fletcher	Republican	2003–

*Law changed to allow governors to succeed themselves. Patton was the first to do so under this law, and only the second governor ever to serve two consecutive terms. The other two-term governor, James Garrard, served from 1796 to 1804.

Presidents of the University of Kentucky*, 1866–2005

Term	President
1866–1867	John Augustus Williams
1868–1869	Joseph Desha Pickett
1869–1910	James K. Patterson
1910–1917	Henry S. Barker
1917–1940	Frank L. McVey
1940 [interim president]	Thomas Poe Cooper
1941–1956	Herman L. Donovan
1956–1963	Frank G. Dickey
1963–1968	John W. Oswald
1968–1970 [interim president]	Albert D. Kirwin
1970–1987	Otis A. Singletary
1987–1989	David P. Roselle
1989–2001	Charles Wethington
2001–	Lee T. Todd, Jr.

*Established as Agricultural and Mechanical (A&M) College of Kentucky in 1865, as a department of Kentucky University (now Transylvania University); in 1878, A&M was separated out from Kentucky University and moved to its primary Lexington campus location on South Limestone Street; in 1908, the name was changed to State University, Lexington, Kentucky; in 1916, the Kentucky General Assembly changed the name to the University of Kentucky.

Administrators and Staff of Lexington Community College and Lexington Technical Institute, 1965–2005

Associate Director/Dean of Academic Affairs

Beatty, Eunice, Ph.D., Kentucky

Blake, Robert, M.A., Kentucky–interim

Boyatt, Iva, M.A., Kentucky–interim

Carey, Sandra, Ph.D., Kent State

Carr, Benjamin, Ph.D., Kentucky

Edwards, Allen, Ph.D., Texas

Jaggard, Sharon, Ph.D., Pennsylvania State

McLaughlin, Judy, M.S., Kentucky–interim

Revell, Leana, Ed.D., Texas

Stice, Patsy, M.A., Murray State–interim

Thomas, Steve

Webb, Carol, M.A., Kentucky–interim

Business Officer/Dean of Business Affairs

Childre, Marilyn, B.B.A., Kentucky

Holt, Dan, M.A., Western Kentucky University

Combs, Ruth, M.B.A., Kentucky

Dean/Vice President/Chancellor of the Community College System

Carr, Benjamin, Ph.D., Kentucky

Hartford, Ellis F., Ed.D., Harvard

Wall, M. Stanley, Ed.D., Kentucky

Wethington, Charles T., Jr., Ph.D., Kentucky

Dean of Student Affairs

Taylor, Paul

Director

Archer, M. L., M.A., Kentucky

Carr, Benjamin, Ph.D., Kentucky–interim

Godbey, Edsel, Ph.D.

Jaggard, Sharon, Ph.D., Pennsylvania State

Price, William N., Ed.D., Arizona State

Wethington, Charles T., Jr., Ph.D., Kentucky

President of the Community College

Chapman, James, Ph.D.–interim

Edwards, Allen, Ph.D., Texas

Friedel, Janice N., Ph.D., Iowa

Kerley, James, Ph.D., Florida State

Newberry, Anthony, Ph.D.–interim

President of the University of Kentucky

Oswald, John, Ph.D., California

Roselle, David, Ph.D., Duke

Singletary, Otis, Ph.D., Louisiana State

Todd, Lee, Ph.D., MIT

Wethington, Charles, Ph.D., Kentucky

Registrar

Clark, Karen

Greissman, Richard

Harp-Stephens, Becky

Lefler, Patricia

Full-Time Tenured Faculty of University of Kentucky Lexington Community College and University of Kentucky Lexington Technical Institute, 1965–2005

Note: Professorial rank listed reflects the highest rank attained as of compilation of this list from available information. Highest degree earned is also a reflection of most recent information available. Discipline at the end of each entry reflects the teaching department or area assigned to the faculty member. Where two or more comparable degrees have been awarded (e.g., Ph.D. and Ed.D., M.A., M.S., and M.A.T.) all are listed. Information compiled from college catalogs, commencement announcements, and from individual sources.

Professor

Allen, Margaret, M.A., Kentucky, 1981; Communications and Women's Studies

Anthony, Joseph, M.A., Long Island, 1979; English

Barber, Cynthia, M.A.T., Kentucky, 1984; Mathematics

Beatty, Eunice, Ph.D., Kentucky, 1994; Dental Hygiene, Educational Psychology and Academic Affairs

Birchfield, Martha, M.L.S., Florida State, 1969; M.A., Florida State, 1969; Library Information Technology

Blake, Robert, M.A., Kentucky, 1974; Engineering Technology

Boyatt, Iva, M.A., Kentucky, 1977; Secretarial/Office Administration

Brady, Barbara, M.S., Louisiana Tech, 1982; Mathematics

Cantrell, Timothy, M.P.A., Western Kentucky, 1988; M.A., Western Kentucky, 1969; History and Political Science

Chiswell, Charles Lawrence, D.M.D., Kentucky, 1972; Dental Hygiene

Coulston, Charles, M.S.Ed., Kentucky, 1995; Nuclear Medicine

Crowley, Lillie, Ph.D., University of Warwick, 2001; Mathematics

Doty, Sarajane, M.S.Ed., Kentucky, 1991; Radiography

Embry, Nolen, M.A., North Alabama, 1979; Psychology

Freed, Michele, M.B.S., Southeastern Oklahoma State, 1977; Developmental Studies

Freyman, Marcia, M.S.L.S., Kentucky, 1989; M.A., George Washington, 1980; Librarian

Frisbie, Elizabeth, Ph.D., Pennsylvania State, 1987; Biology

Gibbs, James, M.L.S., Kentucky, 1987; M.A., Kentucky, 1982; History and Philosophy

Goode, James, M.A.Ed., Kentucky, 1971; English

Gornto, Robin, M.S.Ed., Kentucky, 1989; Dental Laboratory Technology

Hicks, Janet, M.A., Kentucky, 1997; M.S.N., Kentucky, 1985; Nursing and English

Hunt, Carol, M.A., Ball State, 1973; English

Jackson, Jean, Ph.D., Sheffield, 1980; Biology

James, Charles, M.L.S., Kentucky, 1992; M.A., Kentucky, 1982; Librarian

Kavanaugh, Susan, M.S.Ed., Kentucky, 1981; Biology

Kelly, Debbie, M.Ed., Cincinnati, 1980; Dental Hygiene

Kolasa, James, M.S., Kentucky, 1994; Computer and Information Technology

Leon, Ana, M.S., Jacksonville State, 1987; Mathematics

Leonard, Cynthia, M.A., Kentucky, 1984; Communications and Women's Studies

Maggard, Sarah, M.B.A., Kentucky, 1983; Accounting

Martin, Diana, M.A., Kentucky, 1990; English

McLaughlin, M. Judy, M.S., Kentucky, 1982; Radiography

Mowbray, Erla, Ph.D., Kentucky, 2000; Nursing

Murphy, Donna, M.H.E., Morehead State, 1982; Counselor

Noffsinger, Anne, Ed.D., Kentucky, 1979; Nursing

Olson-Biglieri, Joanne, M.A., Bowling Green, 1984; M.A., Syracuse, 1976; Spanish and French

Pagan, Bonnie, M.A., Kentucky, 1988; M.A., Morehead State, 1976; English, Communications and Women's Studies

Partin, Vicki, M.S., Kentucky, 1981; Mathematics

Richardson, Kathleen, M.A.L.S., Rosary College, 1983; Librarian

Ripley, Michael Bret, M.S., Eastern Kentucky, 1990; History

Roberts, Francis, III, M.S.Ed., Kentucky, 1981; Respiratory Care and Academic Affairs

Robertson, Marshall, M.A., Kentucky, 1984; Accounting

Rutledge, Judy, M.A., Kentucky, 1969; Counselor

Saunier, Margaret, Ph.D., Kentucky, 1987; Mathematics

Scorsone, Analy, Ph.D., Texas, 1990; Mathematics

Shear, Donald A., Dental Laboratory Technology

Singleton, Debbie, M.A.Ed., Kentucky, 1977; Mathematics

Spence, Agnes S., Counselor

Spencer, Janella, M.S.Ed., Kentucky, 1992; Dental Hygiene

Stice, Patsy, M.A., Murray State, 1971; Secretarial/Office Administration and Accounting Technology

Subramanian, Seetha, M.Sc., London, 1972; Physics

Wachtel, David, Ph.D., SUNY, Buffalo, 1983; Sociology

Walker, Charlene, M.A., Eastern Kentucky, 1988; Counselor

Webb, Carol, M.A., Kentucky, 1965; Secretarial/Office Administration

White, Barbara, M.A., Kentucky, 1978; Business Management Technology

Wilson, Vicki Kegley, M.A., Kentucky, 1982; Communications

Womack, Becky, M.A., Mississippi, 1975; English

Zoll, Gregory, M.S.Ed., Kentucky, 1995; Dental Laboratory Technology

Associate Professor

Abel, Eileen, Ph.D., Tennessee, 1995; English

Adkins, Michael, M.S., Missouri, 1980; Economics

Austin, Vincent, Ph.D., Kentucky, 1994; Biology

Ball, Andrew, M.A., Kentucky, 1988; English

Batson, William, M.Arch., Ohio State, 1995; Architectural Technology

Beam, Carolyn, Secretarial Administration

Binzer, Michael, B.S., Cincinnati, 1987; Engineering Technology

Blankenship, Paul, M.S., West Virginia, 1990; Mathematics

Boes, Donald, M.F.A., Indiana, 1985; English

Carey, Sandra, Ph.D., Kent State, 1979; English and Academic Affairs

Carlton, Heather, M.S.N., Kentucky, 1999; Nursing

Carpenter, Gail, M.S.N., Kentucky, 1978; Nursing

Carr, Sharon, M.A., Kentucky, 1986; Information Management and Design

Carroll, Cynthia, M.S., Eastern Kentucky, 1992; Computer Aided Design

Chirwa, Robert, M.S., Kentucky, 1990; Computer and Information Technology

Chittenden, David, M.B.A., Kentucky, 1971; Business

Connell, James J., Electrical Engineering

Cothran, Marian, M.S., Oklahoma, 1978; Biology

Dameron, Arthur, M.S.Ed., Kentucky, 1987; Dental Laboratory Technology

Dickison, Kathy, M.A., Kentucky, 1976; English

East, Paul, M.S., Kentucky, 1981; Mathematics

Eldridge, Brent, M.S., Tennessee, 1992; Chemistry

Elzey-Miller, Barbara, M.A., Kentucky, 1997; Mathematics

Fairchild, Virginia, M.B.A., Eastern Kentucky, 1993; Business

Famularo, Joy, M.A., Kentucky, 1966; English

Feeney, Greg, Ph.D., Kentucky, 1999; Communications

Flanary, Patricia, M.A., Eastern Kentucky, 1971; English

Floyd, Ninfa, M.A.Ed., Morehead State, 1990; Spanish

Fluker, Otis, Counselor

Foster, Chester, Engineering Graphics

Fuhrmann, John, Dental Laboratory Technology

Galvin, Sarah, M.A., Murray State, 2005; M.A., Kentucky, 1993; Developmental Studies

Gard, O. W., M.S., Georgia Institute of Technology, 1952; Mechanical Engineering Technology

Gil, Caroline, M.S., Massachusetts Institute of Technology, 1993; M.Sc., Toronto, 1988; Chemistry

Glasscock, Rebecca, Ph.D., Kentucky, 2004; Geography

Gooch, Peyton, M.S., Kentucky, 1975; Nursing

Graves, Jacqueline Sherrard, M.S.N., Kentucky, 1995; Nursing

Guiseppi, Lori, M.A.Ed., Kentucky, 1993; English

Hackney, Sandra, A.A.S., Lexington Community College, 1996; A.A.S., Lexington Technical Institute, 1983; Real Estate

Hammond, Robert, M.S., Indiana, 1958; Business Technology

Hardwick, Donald, M.B.A., Xavier, 1981; Business

Hobbs, Rebecca, Dental Hygiene

Hollingsworth, Randolph, M.A.T., Colgate, 1981; History and Women's Studies

Holt, Daniel, M.A., Western Kentucky, 1972; History

Holt, Deborah, M.S., Kentucky, 1995; Computer and Information Technology

Hopper, Kevin, Ph.D., Kentucky, 1998; Biology

Houghton-Estes, Lori, M.A., Eastern Kentucky, 1995; English

Humble, Jeanne, M.A., Kentucky, 1970; Sociology and Anthropology

Ingle, Cynthia, M.S., Eastern Kentucky, 1987; Psychology

Isert, Joseph W., Real Estate

Jupin, Arvin, Ph.D., Kentucky, 1978; English

Justice, Laura, M.S.Ed., Kentucky, 2000; Dental Hygiene

Kalala, Nkongolo, Ph.D., Kentucky, 1995; Economics

Kelly, Ryan, M.S., Florida State, 1995; Geography

Kemper, John T., A.A.S., Southern Illinois, 1964; Dental Laboratory Technology

King, Richard, M.S., Kentucky, 1994; Computer and Information Technology

Knowles, Tracy, M.S., Indiana, 1998; Chemistry

LaFontaine, Lucy, M.S., Kentucky, 1994; Radiography

Lane, Leon, M.A., Kentucky, 1993; Anthropology and Sociology

Lanier, Rebecca, M.S.Ed., Kentucky, 1992; Mathematics

Lefler, Patricia, Ph.D., Indiana, 2004; Psychology

Lenning, Kristan, M.S., Indiana, 1983; M.A.T., Vanderbilt, 1972; Chemistry

Liles, Tammy, M.S., Kentucky, 1994; M.S., Morehead State, 1987; Biology

Linder, Jacqueline, M.A., Sonoma State, 1985; English

Long, Betty Weeks, B.Arch., Kentucky, 1978; Architectural Technology

Luyster, William, M.A.T., Louisville, 1990; Physics and Astronomy

Magee, David, M.B.A., Cincinnati, 1981; Business Technology

Maggard, Robert, M.S., South Dakota School of Mines and Technology, 1967; Physics

Matchuny, James, M.S., Kentucky, 1996; Respiratory Care

McDermott, Patrick, Dental Laboratory Technology

Miller, Patricia, M.A.Ed., Kentucky, 1994; Information Management and Design

Miller-Massey, Pat A., M.S.Ed., Kentucky, 1996; Radiography

Miriti, Landrea, M.A., Montclair State, 1988; Mathematics

Molloy, Lynn, M.A.T., North Carolina, 1966; Mathematics

Mueller, Chad, M.S., Colorado, 1995; Chemistry

Mullins, Larry, M.S., Eastern Kentucky, 1973; Mathematics

Murphy, William Kevin, M.B.A., Kentucky, 1991; Architectural Technology

Norman, Valiant, M.S., Montana State, 1974; Geography

Otiento, Iddah, M.A., Eastern Kentucky, 2001; English

Ott, J. Stephen, M.A., Kentucky, 1988; Mathematics

Papanicolaou, Thomas, M.S., Kentucky, 1994; Computer and Information Technology

Pelfrey, Holly, M.S.Ed., Kentucky, 1993; Mathematics

Perry, Kenneth, M.S., Murray State, 1975; Engineering Graphics

Phillips, James W., Data Processing

Phillips, Joseph W., Librarian

Puckett, Russell E., M.S., Kentucky, 1959; Electrical Engineering Technology

Ramsey, Tammy, M.F.A., Spaulding, 2004; M.A., Kentucky, 1988; English and Journalism

Risk, Carol Taylor, Developmental Studies

Robison, Janet, M.S., Western Kentucky, 1981; Biology

Rogers, Thomas, B.Arch., Kentucky, 1986; B.S., Eastern Kentucky, 1981; Architectural Technology

Roser, Lynn, M.S.N., Kentucky, 1998; Nursing

Ross-Brown, Kimberly, M.A., Nebraska,1996; Communications

Roussos, Panagiotis, M.A., Kentucky, 1988; Economics

Sadat, Anas, M.S., Marshall, 1998; Computer and Information Technology

Sanders, Jacqueline, Accounting

Santana, Gary, M.S., Kentucky, 1991; Counselor

Schuman, Daniel, Ph.D., Kentucky, 2002; Philosophy

Scott, John, M.A., Eastern Kentucky, 1990; English

Secrist, Scott R., Nuclear Medicine

Sills, Joe Fred, Ph.D., North Carolina, 1964; Community Health

Slone, LaVerne, Nursing

Smoot, Rick, Ph.D., Kentucky, 1988; History

Story, John, Psy.D., Forest Institute, 1991; Psychology

Strobel, Norman, Ph.D., Cornell, 1989; Biology

Swanson, Sandra, B.S.Ed., Central Missouri State, 1970; Computer Information Systems

Swetnam, Bruce, B.Arch., Kentucky, 1979; Architectural Technology

Taghizadeh, Rasoul, M.S., Kentucky, 1989; Accounting

Thacker, Teresa, M.S.N., Kentucky, 1993; Nursing

Travelbee, Cynthia Norman, M.S., Texas Christian, 1988

Underwood, Dale, M.Ed., Memphis State, 1970; Computer Science

Walker, Robert, M.S., Eastern Kentucky, 1979; Engineering Graphics

Wasielewski, Ronald, M.S.Ed., Kentucky, 1981; Respiratory Care

Watts, Jean, M.E.M., Duke, 1987; Environmental Science Technology

Webster-Little, Stacy, M.A., Nebraska, 1996; Communications

Weeks, Betty B., Architectural Technology

Weill, Lawrence, Ph.D., Kentucky, 1987; Developmental Studies

Wethington, Charles, Ph.D., Kentucky, 1966; President Emeritus of the University of Kentucky

White, Steven J., Ph.D., Illinois, 1990; History

Whitescarver, Shirley, Ph.D., Kentucky, 1987; Nursing

Wilson, Davis B., Secretarial Administration

Worth, Ben, Ph.D., Kentucky, 2004; English

Wyatt, Nelda, Ed.D., Kentucky, 1999; History

Yonts, Linda, M.S.N., Kentucky, 1985; Nursing

Technical Programs, 2004–2005

Source: Lexington Community College Catalog, 2004–2005

Architectural Technology
Business Technology
Civil Engineering Technology
Computer Information Systems
Dental Hygiene
Dental Laboratory Technology
Early Childhood Education

Engineering Technology
Environmental Science Technology
Information Management and Design
Nuclear Medicine Technology
Nursing
Radiography
Respiratory Care

Certificate Programs, 2004–2005

Geographic Information Systems Technology
Library Information Technology

LCC Clubs and Organizations, 2004–2005

Academic Team

AIAS: American Institute
of Architecture Students

Athena Club

College Democrats

College Republicans

International Association of
Administrative Professionals

Dental Lab

International Students' Club

Kentucky Association
of Nursing

Phi Theta Kappa

Students in Free Enterprise
(SIFE)

SADHA: Student American
Dental Hygienist Association

Student Government
Association

Student Organization
of Radiographics

SWAT: Student Service,
Work and Training Team

UNITY

Lexington Community College
Alumni Association Charter Board Members

Joyce Beatty
Sabrina Blake
Guy Cornish
Rebecca Flanagan

John Fuhrmann
Cathie Hill
Sara Holroyd
Debbie Holt
Kathryn Hunt

Judy McLaughlin
Betsy Strother
Patricia Tucci
Harriet Hillenmeyer Strode

Lexington Community College
Outstanding Staff Award, 1999–2005

1999	2000	2001	2002
Beverly Drake	Veronica Miller	Ethelene Denissoff	Melissa Elliott
Kelly Bevins	Karen Mayo	Angie Fielder	Carmolyn Back
Ginger Porter	Leona Dunn	Shelbie Hugle	Sally Soard
Rick Rydz	Dianalee Crone	Linda Mudge	Andrea Sanford
Sydney Basehart	Linda Faul	Terry Tipton	Shannon Bentley

2003	2004	2005
Dianalee Crone	Michael Ball	Ray Forsythe
Regina Johnson	Nancy Dixon	Becky Harp-Stevens
Jessica Hayden	Kathe Proctor	Harold Lightsey
Tania Crawford	Christy Terry	Karen Murtiff
Julie McClanahan	Della White	Tammy Satterly

Distinguished Alumni, 1992–2005
Lexington Community College

Year	Name	Year	Name
1992	Dr. Sandra L. Frazier	1999	John Fuhrmann
1993	Virginia L. Lawson	2000	Karen S. Hill
1994	Joyce S. Beatty	2001	John T. Slugantz II
1995	Debbie L. Holt	2002	Rob Culbertson
1996	Dr. Carolyn O'Daniel	2003	Faith Faulkner
1997	Dianne Loggins	2004	Guy Cornish
1998	Lawrence C. Davis	2005	Glenna Fletcher

Lexington Community College
Outstanding Teacher Award, 2001–04

2001	2002	2003	2004
Becky Lanier Bill Luyster Vicki Partin Shirley Whitescarver Sean Mullaney Cheri Sullivan	Toni Ann Mills Ryan Kelly Kimberly Ross-Brown Charlene Walker Ninfa Floyd Robin Taylor	Debbie Stoops Kevin Hopper Beth Healander Vicki Wilson Diana Martin	Kristin Leaning Sarajane Doty Ryan Kelly Russell Moore Juliana McDonald Jill Meek

Dr. Anne Noffsinger Nursing Award, 1981–2005

Year	Recipient	Year	Recipient
1981	Barbara Hendren	1993	Patricia Tucci
1982	Marsha Peters	1994	Anita Capillo and Susan Champ
1983	Teresita Alonso	1995	Patricia Shaffer
1984	Diana Frankenberger	1996	Ruth Branton and Dora Saylor
1985	Anne Roberts	1997	Dorthea Corman
1986	Mary Dick	1998	Eileen Lindsey
1987	Sunny Mooney	1999	Tina Wallace
1988	Victor Wood	2000	Galisa Watts and Shannon French
1989	Laurie Adcock-Oliver	2001	Carmen Galloway-Spencer
1990	Nancy Claycomb	2003	Debra Elgaouni
1991	Donna Clifford	2004	Tammy Conley
1992	Mona Abbott and Kay Wilson	2005	Carolyn Barbera

Chosen by Nursing faculty and students, the award is given to that person or persons seen as the epitome of a nurse and caregiver. It is given to the person whom the faculty and student body would choose as one's own or one's family's nurse and caregiver.

Not Awarded in 2002.

Carolyn Beam Faculty Award, 1990–2005

1990–91	Sarah Maggard		1998–99	Carol Hunt
1991–92	Peggy Saunier		1999–2000	Becky Womack
1992–93	Iva Dean Boyatt		2000–01	Charles James
1993–94	Dale N. Underwood		2001–02	Pat Miller
1994–95	Charles Coulston		2002–03	Donna Murphy
1995–96	Randolph Hollingsworth		2003–04	Rebecca Glasscock
1996–97	Joanne Olson-Biglieri		2004–05	Erla Mowbray
1997–98	Jan Hicks			

Scholarship Awards Lexington Community College

Bennett-Allen Book Scholarship	Commonwealth Scholarship	Community Scholarship	Don Shear Scholarship	Dr. Helen M. Reed Book Scholarship
Dr. Jack B. Jordan Scholarship	Gordon M. Nichols Scholarship	Hazel Q. Berryman Memorial Scholarship	John T. Smith Scholarship	Kentucky Colonel Better Life Scholarship
Lewis E. Owens Scholarship	Marilyn Childre Scholarship	Mosaic Scholarship	N. O. Kimbler Memorial Scholarship	President's Scholarship
Presidential Scholarship	Stanley H. McGowan II Book Scholarship	The Lexington Rotary Club Scholarship	Timothy A. Cantrell Scholarship	Todd Lewis Musgrave Memorial Scholarship
Tony Tombasco Scholarship	*Note: Awards made in various years over the life of the College. Many of the awards listed are program-specific.*			

LTI/LCC Disability Support Services
Student Data, 1976–2005*

Fiscal Year	Students with disabilities	Students with learning disabilities	Graduates with disabilities
1976–77	17		
1977–78	19		
1981–82	100		
1985–86	163		
1992–93	297		
1993–94	415	19%	
1994–95	370	19%	20
1995–96	583	23%	26
1996–97	396	23%	27
1997–98	337**	27.5%	38
1998–99			
1999–2000	426	27%	32
2000–01	328	33.5%	33
2001–02	410	36%	
2002–03	354	46%	33
2003–04	412	47%	40
2004–05	414	50%	39

*Data between 1976 and 1994 is sporadic, but does indicate continuous growth in the number of students with disabilities on campus. Blank spaces indicate where data was *unavailable*.

**Decrease attributed to changes in funding by Kentucky Department of Vocational Rehabilitation (DVR). Previously, more than two-thirds of students with disabilities were sponsored by DVR; for 1997-98 only 50 percent received DVR funding to attend Lexington Community College. Students served also had more severe disabilities paralleling changes made by DVR regarding their federal mandate to serve the most severely disabled individuals.

All data in this table was made available courtesy of Ms. Veronica Miller.

Actual Operating Expenditures, 1968–1985
University of Kentucky Lexington Technical Institute and University of Kentucky Lexington Community College

Source: University of Kentucky Community College System, Compendium of Selected Data & Characteristics, various years and issues.

Year	Expenditures
1968–69	$134,266
1970–71	210,911
1971–72	204,053
1972–73	254,487
1973–74	378,753
1974–75	438,251
1975–76	549,836

Year	Expenditures
1976–77	895,781
1977–78	1,028,821
1978–79	1,313,190
1979–80	1,465,149
1980–81	1,836,269
1981–82	2,048,671
1984–85	3,457,044

Total Operating Expenses, 1990–91 to 2003–04
University of Kentucky Lexington Community College

Source: Information provided courtesy of Ms. Marilyn Childre.

Year	Expenditures
1990–91	$11,283,056
1991–92	13,951,638
1992–93	14,649,185
1993–94	14,973,660
1994–95	15,505,241
1995–96	15,889,749
1996–97	17,654,328

Year	Expenditures
1997–98	19,207,622
1998–99	20,882,090
1999–2000	24,056,685
2000–01	27,852,789
2001–02	24,280,999
2002–03	26,312,207
2003–04	28,216,311

Lexington and Fayette County, Kentucky, Population Statistics, 1790–2005

Year	Population
1790	834
1800	1,795
1810	4,325
1820	5,279
1830	6,026
1840	6,997
1850	8,159
1860	9,321

Year	Population
1870	14,801
1880	16,656
1890	21,567
1900	26,369
1910	35,099
1920	41,534
1930	45,736
1940	49,304

Year	Population
1950	55,534
1960	62,810
1970	108,137
1980	204,165
1990	225,366
2000	260,512
2005	268,080

Source: United States Census data.

Entries from 1790 to 1970 are of the city of Lexington proper. Post-1980 entries indicate the unified Lexington-Fayette Urban County Government population.

Fayette County, Kentucky, Population, 1900–2000

Year	Population
1900	42,071
1910	47,715
1920	54,664
1930	68,543
1940	78,899
1950	100,746

Year	Population
1960	131,906
1970	174,323
1980	204,165
1990	225,366
2000	260,512

Source: "The Uncommon Wealth," Register of the Kentucky Historical Society 101 (Summer 2003): 239.

University of Kentucky Lexington Technical Institute
Headcount Enrollment by Year, 1965–83

Year	Number Enrolled
1965	20*
1966	76
1967	112
1968	174
1969	232
1970	586

Year	Number Enrolled
1971	750
1972	863
1973	1,118
1974	1,281
1975	1,654
1976	1,765

Year	Number Enrolled
1977	2,030
1978	1,867
1979	2,074
1980	2,111
1981	2,306
1982	2,462
1983	2,532

Sources: University of Kentucky Community College System, Compendium of Selected Data & Characteristics 1974-75, 1982-83, 1985-86

* *This number from narrative report,* University of Kentucky Lexington Technical Institute Self-Study Report, *August 1980.*

University of Kentucky Lexington Community College
Headcount Enrollment by Year, 1984–2005

Year	Number Enrolled
1984	2,573
1985	2,538
1986	2,587
1987	2,995
1988	3,401
1989	3,928
1990	4,588

Year	Number Enrolled
1991	4,985
1992	4,862
1993	5,046
1994	5,018
1995	5,248
1996	5,520
1997	5,609

Year	Number Enrolled
1998	6,124
1999	6,828
2000	7,214
2001	7,793
2002	8,290
2003	8,672
2004	8,808
2005	8,312

Sources: University of Kentucky Community College System, Compendium of Selected Data & Characteristics 1991-92; *UK Lexington Community College,* Factbook 1999-2000; *Bluegrass Community and Technical College,* Factbook 2005 *online*

Archival and Collected Materials

Responses to the Call for Papers [in celebration of the 25th anniversary of the community college system]. Lexington: Community College System, University of Kentucky, 1988–89.

University of Kentucky Community College System. *Compendium of Selected Data & Characteristics,* various years. Dr. A. J. Hauselman and Dan Tudor, eds. November 1986.

University of Kentucky Lexington Community College. "Institutional Self-Study 1990."

University of Kentucky Lexington Community College. "Institutional Self-Study 2000."

University of Kentucky Lexington Community College Transition Committee. "Lexington Community College: A New Relationship with the University of Kentucky." October 31, 1997.

University of Kentucky, Lexington, Special Collections and Archives, Margaret I. King Library.

University of Kentucky Lexington Technical Institute. "Institutional Self-Study 1980."

University of Kentucky Special Collections and Archives, King Library, Lexington.

Books

American Council on Education. *College Students Today: A National Portrait.* Washington, D.C.: November 2005.

Baiocco, Sharon A., and Jamie N. DeWaters. *Successful College Teaching: Problem-Solving Strategies of Distinguished Professors.* Boston: Allyn and Bacon, 1998.

Baker, George A., III. *A Handbook on the Community College in America: Its History, Mission, and Management.* Westport, Conn.: Greenwood Press, 1994.

Bledstein, Burton J. *The Culture of Professionalism: The Middle Class and the Development of Higher Education in America.* New York: W. W. Norton, 1976.

Brint, Steven, and Jerome Karabel. *The Diverted Dream: Community Colleges and the Promise of Educational Opportunity in America, 1900–1985.* New York: Oxford University Press, 1989.

Cohen, Arthur M., and Florence B. Brawer. *The American Community College.* 4th ed. San Francisco: Jossey-Bass, 2003.

Cone, Carl. *The University of Kentucky: A Pictorial History.* Lexington: University Press of Kentucky, 1989.

Cox, Dwayne D., and William J. Morison. *The University of Louisville.* Lexington: University Press of Kentucky, 2000.

Davis, L. Mitchell. *Desirable Characteristics of and Criteria for Establishing A System of Community Colleges in Kentucky.* Commonwealth of Kentucky Department of Education. Educational Bulletin 34, No. 1, January 1966.

Dougherty, Kevin J. *The Contradictory College: The Conflicting Origins, Impacts, and Futures of the Community College.* Albany: State University of New York Press, 1994.

Eaton, Judith S., ed. *Women in Community Colleges.* New Directions for Community Colleges, Arthur M. Cohen and Florence B. Brawer, eds. No. 34, 1981. San Francisco: Jossey-Bass, 1981.

Ellis, William E. *A History of Eastern Kentucky University: The School of Opportunity.* Lexington: University Press of Kentucky, 2005.

Felnagle, Richard. *Maricopa's Community Colleges: The Turbulent Evolution of an Education Giant.* Seattle: Elton-Wolf, 2000.

Fifty Years of the University of Kentucky African-American Legacy 1949–1999. Lexington: University of Kentucky, 1999.

Grubb, W. Norton, with Helena Worthen, Barbara Byrd, Elnora Webb, Norena Badway, Chester Case, Stanford Goto, and Jennifer Curry Villeneuve. *Honored But Invisible: An Inside Look at Teaching in Community Colleges.* New York: Routledge, 1999.

Bibliography

Harrell, Kenneth E., ed. *The Public Papers of Governor Edward T. Breathitt 1963–1967*. Lexington: University Press of Kentucky, 1984.

Harvey, William B., and James Valadez, eds. *Creating and Maintaining a Diverse Faculty*. New Directions for Community Colleges, Arthur M. Cohen and Florence B. Brawer, eds. No. 87, Fall 1994. San Francisco: Jossey-Bass, 1994.

Higginbottom, George, and Richard M. Romano, eds. *Curriculum Models for General Education*. New Directions for Community Colleges, Arthur M. Cohen and Florence B. Brawer, eds. No. 92, Winter 1995. San Francisco: Jossey-Bass, 1995.

Hoptown: Hopkinsville, Christian County, Kentucky. The Mountain Workshops, 2001.

Lucas, Christopher J. *American Higher Education: A History*. New York: St. Martin's, 1994.

Marsden, George M. *The Soul of the American University: From Protestant Establishment to Established Nonbelief*. New York: Oxford, 1994.

Southern Association of Colleges and Schools. *Proceedings*. Vol. 55, no. 1, April 2003. Decatur, Ga.: Southern Association of Colleges and Schools, 2003.

Sykes, Charles J. *Dumbing Down Our Kids: Why America's Children Feel Good About Themselves but Can't Read, Write, or Add*. New York: St. Martin's, 1995.

Thelin, John R. *A History of American Higher Education*. Baltimore: The Johns Hopkins University Press, 2004.

University of Kentucky: Then and Now. Louisville: Harmony House, 1993.

Zwerling, L. Steven, ed. *The Community College and Its Critics*. New Directions for Community Colleges, Arthur M. Cohen and Florence B. Brawer, eds. No. 54, June 1986. Jossey-Bass Higher Education Series. San Francisco: Jossey-Bass, 1986.

Newspapers

Advocate-Messenger, Danville, Kentucky
Harrodsburg (Kentucky) Herald
Kentucky Kernel [University of Kentucky]
Lexington Community College Courier
Lexington Herald-Leader

Oral History Interviews

Conducted by John D. Adams:

Marilyn Childre
Otis Fluker, Jr.
Dan Holt
Marie L. Piekarski
Francis Roberts III
Paul Taylor

Conducted by Rick Smoot:

Peter P. Bosomworth, M.D.
Larry Chiswell
Jim Kerley
Cindy Leonard
Pat McDermott
Peggy Saunier

Other interview material:

John W. Oswald, interviewed by Terry Birdwhistell, August 10, 1987, transcript, Oral History Program, Special Collections and Archives, King Library, University of Kentucky.

John W. Oswald, interviewed by Terry Birdwhistell, August 11, 1987, transcript, Oral History Program, Special Collections and Archives, King Library, University of Kentucky.

John W. Oswald, interviewed by Terry Birdwhistell, August 12, 1987, transcript, Oral History Program, Special Collections and Archives, King Library, University of Kentucky.

John W. Oswald, interviewed by Rick Smoot, November 25, 1985, transcript, University of Kentucky Medical Center Oral History Project, Oral History Program, Special Collections and Archives, King Library, University of Kentucky.

Charles T. Wethington, Jr., interviewed by Rick Smoot, Summer 2007, in personal files.

Unpublished Manuscripts

Porter, Julia Damron. "Factors Associated with Change in Educational Aspirations in University of Kentucky Community Colleges." Unpublished Ed.D. diss., University of Kentucky, 1982.

Stanley, Larry Douglas. "The Historical Development of the Two-Year Colleges in Kentucky 1903–1964." Unpublished Ph.D. diss., University of Kentucky, Lexington, 1974.

Index

About the Author

Richard Clayton Smoot is a native of Ashland, Kentucky, where he attended the public schools and graduated from Paul G. Blazer Senior High School. Rick, pictured above with his late, great canine companion Heffner, holds a liberal arts bachelor's degree in history and a master's degree in history from Marshall University, and earned the doctor of philosophy degree in history from the University of Kentucky. Presently, he is an associate professor of history with Bluegrass Community and Technical College in Lexington, and teaches history in an adjunct capacity at the University of Kentucky. He is author of *Lexington Country Club: A History of the First One Hundred Years, 1901–2001*, published by Donning in 2004, and a co-author and compiler of *Kentucky Through the Centuries* (Kendall/Hunt, 2005).

COURIER

Lexington *Community College*

ablished 1998 Volume 7, Number 7   November 2002

..ayor With Class

..ngton **Mayor-elect** Teresa Isaac talks

..ollege celebrate ..art-time instructo

..CLAY WHITE
..urier Staff

..CC now has a friend in high places.

..n Nov. 5 Theresa Isaac, who for seven year.. a dedicated member of the LCC staff, was ..ayor of Lexington. The following Friday.. honored with a reception in the main hallwa.. ..swald building.

..ayor-elect Isaac was surrounded by student.. w faculty members in a festival of handsh.. and well-wishing.

..his warm environment and interaction betw.. ..nts and faculty are several of the things Ma..

Winchester gives land for LCC site

By DENNIS BERRY
Courier Staff

Lexington Community College has received an early Christmas gift of 20 acres donated by the Industrial Authority of Winchester, paving the way for construction.. center.

"It's a red letter day for.. President Jim Kerley, calling th.. school history.

LCC has had a presence in W.. than 10 years, but the announce.. tion is one that has been years..

"Dr. Kerley and I have be.. project for about four years.. Kerrick, director of Economi.. the industrial authority in Clar.. vision that we both shared."

The donation became p.. Industrial Authority bought 30.. industrial park in Winchester.. the need for higher education to..

"In order to achieve econ.. have to have the education. Th.. ple in our community and help.. es and higher paying jobs," he..

While Kerley and Kerrick l.. LCC in Winchester, Dr. San.. dean of Academic Affairs, rem.. ning of the partnership. We sta.. single class in the basement of.. we moved to one of the local h..

Cont..

Spring Fling has global flair

BY BRIAN QUINN
STAFF REPORTER

The third year of LCC's Spring Fling is bringing a bit of international flavor to campus. On April 18 from noon to three in the afternoon, 14 student organizations with the help of LCC faculty will put on an event to help bring the LCC community together outside the classroom setting. The event will be held outside in the courtyard area with free food, drinks, music, entertainment, leis and prizes.

Aside from the traditional hot dogs and hamburgers, this year there will be a small display of ethnic foods. Local eateries..

ROTC program now open to.. offers chance to practice tea..

BY REID HURLEY
..EDITOR

The media-driven world in which we live often blurs the line between reality, television and movies. They've given us a picture of the army .. testosterone -driven men with chips .. on their shoulder. Not so with the University of Kentucky Army ROTC .rogram.

Drill-sergeants won't be screaming degrad.. ..ng obscenity laced tirades .. cadets, and officers won't..

junior year, provided you have not yet signed a contract or accepted a scholarship, you have no future responsibility to the military. Furthermore, many Army ROTC graduates choose to go on to the National Guard or Army Reserves. No matter where you serve your post-graduation time, you will do so as a commissioned officer.

LCC sophomore Joe Henderson has been part..

> The ROTC requires dedication in the

Academic team wins tourney at ho..

BY FERRAN ROBINSON
CO-EDITOR

The LCC Academic Team won the second tournament of the semester on October 14 with a clean sweep of the competition in front of a home crowd.

The six-member team is comprised of LCC students James Hall, Rick Hayes, Robert Murray, Rebel Solomon, Barret Webb and Dan Whittaker.

LCC placed first in the tournament with 195 points. EKU was second with a score of 185. Georgetown College took third with 183 points. Ohio University and Jefferson Community College Southwest finished fourth and fifth, respectively.

Four academic tournaments are held each semester. The team

Photo by David Hardy
The LCC Academic Team faces off against Transy in the second round of the October 14 tournament.

tied for second in the previous tournament at Georgetown College. After a tie-breaking round,

the team took home a third place trophy.

The Academic Team's mem-

bers are part of a .. LCC student can j.. faculty coaches an.. Larry Mullins, and..

An academic to.. cally involves six .. petition. There are .. each round with 20 toss-up.. tions per half. The questions .. from 5 categories: mathem.. natural science, humanities, .. sciences and general know..

The LCC team belong.. 16-team league made up .. Kentucky schools and 2 s.. from Ohio. LCC is in divis.. of the league.

The next league tourn.. will be held at Pikeville Co.. nity College on Novemb.. where LCC will defend its .. place status.

..lumni Association offers benefits to LCC grads

COURTNEY HAMMONS
..AFF REPORTER

As graduation draws near for .. class of 2002, these students will ..ome LCC alumni with a free-one .r membership to the Lexington ..mmunity College Alumni Associa- ..n whether they decide to be active .he organization or not.

Although it does not fit all cri- ..a of an official association, this ..liate club has named itself an as- ..iation since at least 1992. Becom-

Membership to the association is available to graduates and alumni.

Members, ranging in numbers from 300 to 350, must pay $10 each year while graduates automatically join for free their first year. The yearly dues go into a fund that later go directly back to each member through parties, refreshments, and door prizes. Other money raised or donated by members goes toward the scholarship fund.

Julie Weidmer, Director of Alumni Affairs, said the goal of the

Although graduates will always be LCC alumni, there are many benefits of becoming and staying an active member of the association. Members receive access to lower arena basketball tickets, check out privileges at the library, and two annual copies of the Alumni News, the official newsletter of this association. Members can participate in the annual LCC Homecoming Tailgate Party and the annual Graduation Pizza Party.

To learn more about the LCC and UK Alumni Associations contact

> ## BENEFITS OF ALUMNI ASSOCIATION MEMBERSHIP
> * the first year is free
> * opportunity to purchase lower-arena basketball tickets
> * participation in the annual graduation pizza party
> * participation in the homecoming tailgate party
> .. ileges
> .. newsletter

..on misconception .. ..hat cadets have to serve .. ..e military upon comple- .. This is only partly true. .. .rogram prior to your

which can take one day or th.. weekend. Whether or not the .. trips are voluntary depends o.. along in the program a studen..

On March 3 the ROT..

Cadets .. spend .. of thei.. on retr.. perform.. challer.. drills. .. such ac.. ties are .. volunta.. peer pr.. does ca..

UK LEXINGTON COMMU.. Establishe..

Stu.. Tern..

..C adjusts to status as lone community college

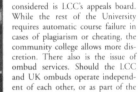

CONTINUED FROM FRONT PAGE

considered is LCC's appeals board. While the rest of the University requires automatic course failure in cases of plagiarism or cheating, the community college allows more discretion. There is also the issue of ombud services. Should the LCC and UK ombuds operate independent of each other, or as part of the same office?

Working with UK

LCC is taking this time of change as an opportunity to strengthen connections between it and the rest of the University.

"We're just in the beginning stages, just beginning to think about what we can do," Kerley said.

Kerley has met with deans, chairs and professors, some of whom were making their first trip across Cooper Drive to LCC.. see, for exam.. ture progra.. College of A..

"My colle.. Lexington C.. more formal .. Community .. opportunity, .. chancellor, .. Campus, said..

about undergraduate research .. engagements for students at vari.. levels of study. It prompts us .. think more comprehensively ab.. work force development for r.. business opportunities – coordi.. ing the education of support pro.. sionals and technicians throu.. LCC with the education .. advanced practitioners .. researchers through the Univer.. System."

With a stronger tie to .. University, Lexington Commun.. College officials also see themsel.. as having a role to play in UK's g.. of becoming a top 20 public in.. tution.

"The missions of the two inst.. tions are different, but they com.. ment each other," said Te.. Arnold, LCC's director of pu.. relations. "On a national level, yo..

ESL sparks conversation

BY CATHERINE NG
ASSISTANT EDITOR

Have you ever stammered in the presence of your classmates and professors because English is not your native language? Or scratched your head while trying to write your English essay? Do not hesitate, the English as a Second Language class (ESL) is what you need.

LCC is providing a program for international students who need to improve their proficiency in English. At the beginning of spring semester 2001, a few LCC faculty members decided to offer an ESL class. It is offered by the LCC International Affairs Action Team to help students from different countries gain confidence in speaking English. ESL at LCC is informal, and it is neither a grammar class nor a writing class.

"The goal of offering an ESL class at LCC is to give international students an environment to speak English," said Sarah Galvin, coordinator of the Development Studies Program. "Instructors normally ask students to..

exchange the ideas in English."

International students come from different cultural backgrounds and speak different native languages. They might be experienced in English grammar, sentence structure and vocabulary; however, conversational English is still a weak point for those who use English as an acquired language.

"As instructors in this program, we always encourage students to discuss their problems that they are facing in English. We try to make a pleasant atmosphere when running the program in class. This can encourage students to speak English. It can also help students to overcome difficulties in English," said Charles Coulston, a nuclear medicine technology professor who has volunteered to help with the ESL class.

According to Coulston, LCC President Dr. Jim Kerley strongly supports the faculty members' making connections with foreign cultures. Six LCC faculty members will make a visit to ..hereby University in Hunan Province,

about American culture and English conversation. ESL at LCC is just one part of this cross-cultural program.

"I ... appreciate that LCC instructors have given us this great opportunity to speak English," said Bell Yakineko, a Japanese sophomore student in psychology major, who is taking the ESL program. "These have understood how international students struggle with a problem in learning English."

The ESL class introduces students to formal and informal English language skills as well as the American .ng and

custom.. process.. sic com.. hension.. ies to r.. opportu.. share t.. new fr.. earth. ..

To clim.. one nee.. riers. F.. who ha.. in any .. 131 and

Multicultural Affairs Office gets the job done

BY FERRAN ROBINSON
CO-EDITOR

Since 1995 the Office of Multicultural Affairs at LCC has been promoting diversity enrichment at LCC. Anthony Hartsfield, a Kentucky State University graduate from Detroit, has been head of the office

..ity population combined with a global post-college work environment, Hartsfield stresses the importance of diversity awareness. He says that the roles of colleges are changing to educate not just academically, but to educate socially with an empha- sis on the appreciation for all cul-

The biggest event in the works for the office is a "major international cultural day" which will take place in the spring. "The event will be a real big gala," says Hartsfield. He says it will be held outdoors and offer LCC students the chance to get

LCC.. BY JOE SCU.. STAFF WRIT..

Septembe.. remembered a.. in this nation'.. At approx..